# HI!

## ANNUAL

## 1992

Printed and Published in Great Britain by
D. C. THOMSON & CO., LTD., 185 Fleet Street,
London EC4A 2HS.

ISBN 0-85116-509-5

Does this look like *your* morning routine? No? Shame on you!

Worry no more, girlies! By turnin' to page 44 you'll find out if your outfit *really* matches your star sign. Should you look like this . . .

. . . or this?

Get ahead with glitter, tinsel 'n' stuff by lookin' at page 114.

Ooh la la! Gen up on Euro lads on page 38.

# inside

**"On the twelfth day of Christmas my true love sent to me . . ." Problem is, Mo doesn't *have* a true love! Can she beat the Christmas rush? See page 66.**

# Hi th

**Hi, it's me, The Ed! You may be wondering what I'm doing introducing this page, but there's a simple answer. You see, during the year some weird and wonderful little notes find their way on to my desk. Normally I'd just ignore them but this time I've decided to let you all have a read — and I'm going to give the Gang some very special goodie bags for their efforts.**

**Now where's that whoopee cushion got to . . .**

## SOAPBOX

**HOW come Liz and Jill are the only members of the "Hi!" Gang to get their photographs in the mag? What about us? We're prettier than them for a start — *and* we've more style. We think the readers would *much* rather see pictures of us and if you don't do something about it we'll . . . we'll . . . cry, probably.**

***Martin and Derek. (Artists.)***

What a touching tale! (Tee, hee!) A goodie bag full of paper hankies is on its way to you — 'cos you'll need 'em to dry your tears!

FOUND this lying on my desk the other day when I came back from lunch.

Dear Ed,

I know it's only two o'clock and I really shouldn't finish until five, but I've just noticed that there's a great new soap starting this afternoon and I simply *must* see it so I can write all about it in "Hi!" next week.

Hope you don't mind.

*The TV Ed.*

P.S. There's a pop prog on too, so I've gone with her. See ya!

*The Pop Ed.*

Well . . . I *wouldn't* mind, but the new soap starts next week! And I don't know *anything* about a pop programme! But what I *do* know is that all our review videos have gone! Oh, well, take a goodie bag full of popcorn and Coke. You can polish it off while you're watching your fave films!

THAT'S it! i've hat enougv! Al i do al day is wok, wirk, wurk! And di i every get any thanks .? Ni! Nit one! (Is this from a Russian — The Ed?). All the other typistsget presents from there magazines * but I don't. Nit ever. Unless you lot stert ti be nicer to me I8m going to stert making lits of mistakes and then yiu'll have something to complain about.' okay,

*Caroline, your typost.*

**P.s. Can i hav an extra big C-Shirt;**

No. But you can have an extra big dictionary and a new typewriter ribbon.

I HATE to say this, but someone has been using my nail varnish again! I know this for a fact, because I put a mark on the bottle last time I used it. The varnish is a bright pink colour, so I'll recognise it at once if I see someone wearing it. Please could you tell everyone that this is *not* to happen again. It's costing me a *fortune,* replacing all that varnish.

*The Beauty Ed.*

Oh — er — this is em, shocking! (Erk! It's difficult to write while you're trying to hide your nails!) I'll certainly speak to everyone. Meanwhile have a goodie bag full of nail varnish — on me!

I HAVE a problem and I don't know what to do about it. You see, I spend all day answering other people's problems but if I had a problem of my own I wouldn't have anyone to answer it for me.

I don't actually *have* a problem, but the problem is, if I *did* have a problem, who would I tell it to? This problem is really getting me down!

*Jill.*

Mmmm! I see the problem (I think)! Have a fabby fun-filled goodie bag containing a wowsome whoopee cushion, a lush(?) laughing bag, some poppin' party tooters and a copy of your all time favourite record — "The Laughing Policeman". That should cheer you up! (I wanted that one — Liz!)

# ere

**Please put your rubbish in the bins provided! This office is a tip!! You have been warned!**
***The cleaner.***

Ooooh! Er — sorry and all that. If you look in the corner beside my desk, you'll find a goodie "bin" filled with all sorts of lovely stuff — like floor polish, dusters and a new apron. Hope you like it!

## SNIPPETS

*WRITERS of Snippets get nothing!*

Please can I have a rise?
***Liz.***

Nope!

Er — em — would you like me to fetch you anything from the canteen?
***Liz.***

Two packets of crisps and a Coke, thanks.

Please can I have a rise?
***Liz.***

Nope!

You're looking really nice today, is that a new outfit?
***Liz.***

Yes! Nice of you to notice.

Please can I have a rise?
***Liz.***

Nope!

Er, has anyone ever told you that you look like Gloria Estefan?
***Liz.***

No, but I've noticed the resemblance myself once or twice.

Can I have a rise?
***Liz.***

No, no, no! (Nope, even!) If you've time to write all these notes, then you don't do enough work! Anyway, it says at the start that writers of Snippets get nothing, so tough!

## CHAPTER ONE

*Mandy had fancied Jon since he joined her class at the beginning of the Easter Term. She loved the way his soft, blond hair flopped forwards over his clear blue eyes and if he so much as smiled she almost melted! He was gorgeous!* ***(Sounds pretty average to me — The Ed.)***

*"I just don't know what to do about it, Jackie," she said to her friend one break. "I don't have the nerve to ask him out myself, but I'll go crazy if I have to put up with any more of this!"* ***(So will I — The Ed! What is this rubbish, anyway?)***

***(Rubbish! Rubbish! It's the start of my new best seller and you shouldn't be reading it — The Fiction Ed.)***

***(And you shouldn't be writing it during working time. Take it back and have an extra special goodie bag — which I'll expect you to fill with ideas for "Hi!" stories! — The Ed!)***

## MATCHMAKERS

**Jill loves Martin! (Tee, hee!)**
***A friend.***

**Oh, Jason! Please ask the Pop Ed out again! That way she might stop gibbering on about the *last* time she met you.**
***A jealous person.***

**S.M. loves M.T. So there!**
***S.M.*** **(Eh?)**

**Shoogie-boogie Dean! Be my Shoogie-boogie baby!**
***The Fashion Ed.***
**(This is ridiculous!)**

**We love "Hi!"**
***The Gang.***

**The Ed loves the Big Boss!**
***Ann Onymous.***

Okay, okay! Enough of that! No goodie bags for these, but if I find out who wrote the last one I'll have a very *special* reward for her!

I HOPE you don't mind me mentioning it, but I think it's time you updated your wardrobe a bit. For starters, you've been wearing that cream shirt ever since I started working on "Hi!" (Not *every* day, I haven't — The Ed.) and, although it *is* nice, it's not exactly *trendy!* Now, if you'd like to come out with me one day I'll help you choose some really hip gear — something that'll wow all the other Editors.

As I said before, I don't like to criticise, but . . .

***The Fashion Ed.***

Ooooh! I'm hurt! That cream shirt was *really* trendy when I bought it. I know it was five years ago, but surely fashions haven't changed all *that* much. But I'll take you up on your offer anyway and you can have a goodie bag full of all my cast offs! They'll certainly look better than that outfit you're wearing today! (That'll teach *her* to criticise her superiors!)

Oh, Tom, you are so wonderful,
You are my one desire.
You'd only have to look at me,
To set my heart on fire.

I've seen you at the cinema,
I've watched you on the telly,
And every time I see you smile,
It turns my legs to jelly.

I love you more than chocolate flakes,
Or Bounty Bar ice-cream!
Oh, Tom, if I don't meet you soon,
I think that I will scream!

**Liz. (Your number one fan!)**

Ooooh! Sweet! For that you *can* have a goodie bag. In fact, I'll give you my own private collection of Tom & Jerry cartoons! (Okay, so I know it isn't *that* Tom she fancies, but you don't expect me to give away my Tom *Cruise* vids, do you?)

**DO you know what I discovered when you were on holiday? Well, I discovered that the Fashion Ed can't spell style! I know this, because when I asked her to write a feature all about style she said she couldn't because she couldn't spell it! I also discovered that the Beauty Ed comes out in spots when she so much as touches make-up, the Pop Ed's gone deaf, the TV Ed's got eye strain, the Fiction Ed's got writer's cramp, the typist's got a sore finger, the artists are allergic to paint and when Liz pops home to feed her dog she doesn't bother coming back again!**

**Then I discovered that, apart from Jill, I was the only one doing any work — and I discovered that I didn't like being a boss! *Please* don't go away again!**

***The Chief Sub Ed!***

Well, I can't promise that, but I will give you a goodie bag which should help. In it you'll find two books. One's called "How To Be A Boss" and the other is "How To Recognise Excuses!". I'm sure you'll find them *very* useful next time I'm on holiday!

Dear Ed,

Can you please pop along to my office some time this morning as there is something I'd like to discuss with you. I would appreciate it if you could call in as soon as possible.

***The Big Boss!***

Oh, certainly, Sir. Right this moment. I won't even finish my coffee.

Sorry, readers, but I'll have to stop now and put on some lipstick. I only hope the Big Boss has a special goodie bag waiting for me — like a huge rise! Keep your fingers crossed for me. 'Bye!

# No Chance!

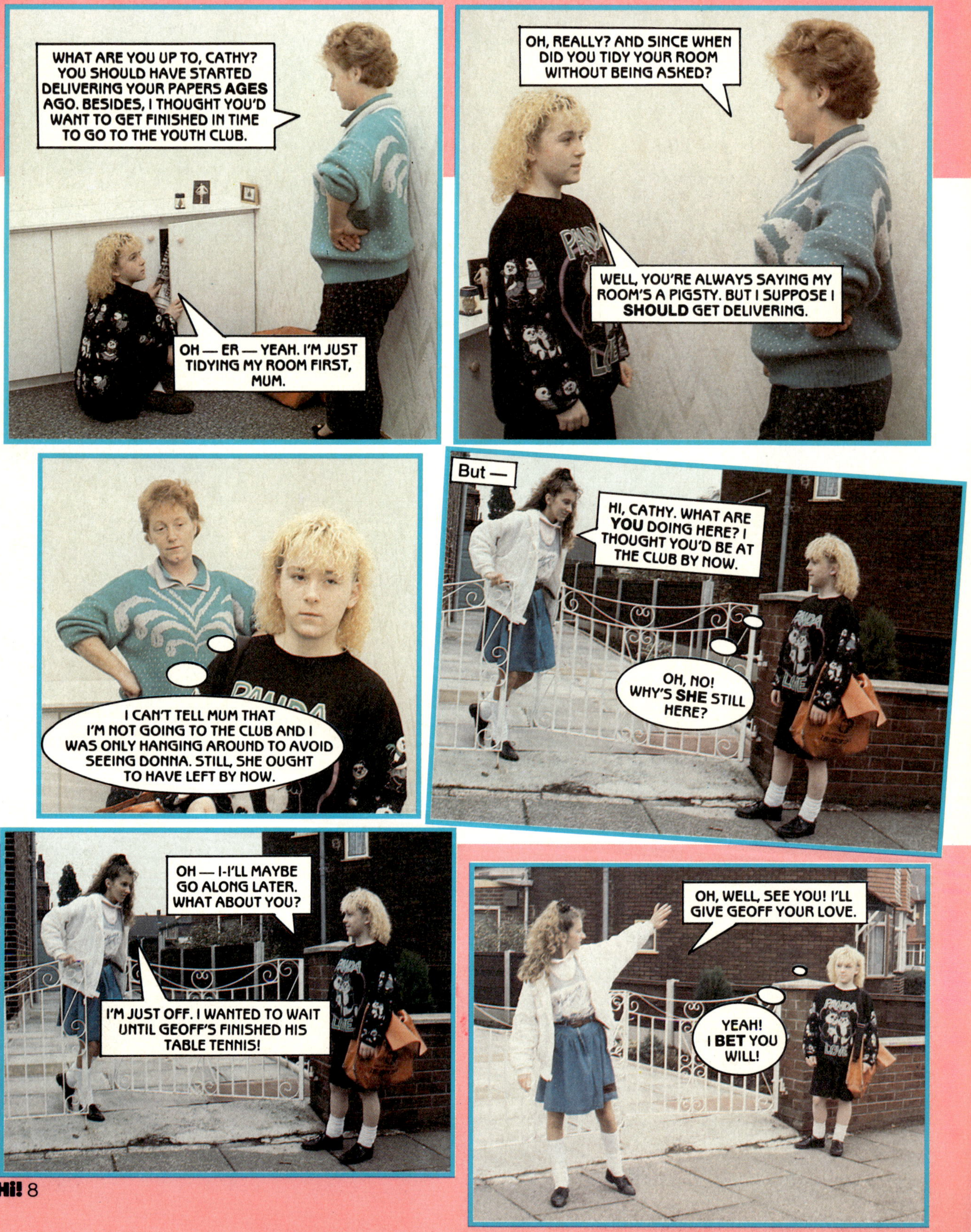

WHAT ARE YOU UP TO, CATHY? YOU SHOULD HAVE STARTED DELIVERING YOUR PAPERS AGES AGO. BESIDES, I THOUGHT YOU'D WANT TO GET FINISHED IN TIME TO GO TO THE YOUTH CLUB.
OH — ER — YEAH. I'M JUST TIDYING MY ROOM FIRST, MUM.
OH, REALLY? AND SINCE WHEN DID YOU TIDY YOUR ROOM WITHOUT BEING ASKED?
WELL, YOU'RE ALWAYS SAYING MY ROOM'S A PIGSTY. BUT I SUPPOSE I SHOULD GET DELIVERING.
I CAN'T TELL MUM THAT I'M NOT GOING TO THE CLUB AND I WAS ONLY HANGING AROUND TO AVOID SEEING DONNA. STILL, SHE OUGHT TO HAVE LEFT BY NOW.
But —
HI, CATHY. WHAT ARE YOU DOING HERE? I THOUGHT YOU'D BE AT THE CLUB BY NOW.
OH, NO! WHY'S SHE STILL HERE?
OH — I-I'LL MAYBE GO ALONG LATER. WHAT ABOUT YOU?
I'M JUST OFF. I WANTED TO WAIT UNTIL GEOFF'S FINISHED HIS TABLE TENNIS!
OH, WELL, SEE YOU! I'LL GIVE GEOFF YOUR LOVE.
YEAH! I BET YOU WILL!

WHY DID SHE HAVE TO PICK ON GEOFF? SHE'S GOT TONS OF FELLAS INTERESTED IN HER — AND I SAW HIM FIRST!
"It was shortly after he moved into No. 24 —"
HI! IS THIS FOR US?
ER — YES.
WOW! HE'S NICE! I HOPE I SEE HIM AGAIN!
"From then on I loved doing my paper round —"
WE'LL HAVE TO STOP MEETING LIKE THIS, YOU KNOW!
HE'S ONLY JOKING, BUT I WISH I COULD MEET HIM SOMEWHERE ELSE!
"And then I did — at the Youth Club. But —"
OH, GREAT SHOT, GEOFF.
IF DONNA FANCIES HIM I'VE GOT NO CHANCE! LIFE'S JUST NOT FAIR!
"And the next night —"
THIS IS A DEAD LOSS. WHEN GEOFF ISN'T TALKING TO DONNA HE'S STARING AT HER. HE HASN'T NOTICED ME FOR WEEKS!
"But then —"
ER — HI, CATHY. I'M GLAD YOU'RE HERE.
WOW! MAYBE THIS IS MY BIG CHANCE AT LAST.

UM . . . IT . . . IT'S ABOUT DONNA. I KNOW SHE'S TALKING TO MIKE, BUT — BUT, WELL, DOES SHE HAVE A REGULAR BOYFRIEND RIGHT NOW?
HOW SHOULD I KNOW? I'M NOT HER SECRETARY!
I MIGHT HAVE KNOWN! SOMETIMES I COULD **KILL** DONNA!
"That was last night —"
SO NOW I CAN'T GO BACK TO THE YOUTH CLUB! I'VE NO CHANCE WITH GEOFF AND I'LL ONLY END UP HATING DONNA IF I SEE THEM THERE TOGETHER. AT LEAST I WON'T SEE HIM TONIGHT ON MY ROUND.
A few nights later —
OH, NO! IT'S GEOFF. I BET HE'S GOING TO GO ON ABOUT HOW GREAT DONNA IS.
HI, CATHY. LOOK, I-I WANTED TO SAY SORRY. I SHOULDN'T HAVE ASKED YOU ABOUT DONNA LIKE THAT. BUT IT WAS PHIL. HE KEPT PESTERING ME TO TRY AND FIND OUT.
YOU — YOU MEAN YOU ASKED FOR **PHIL?**
YEAH — HE'S GOING TO ASK HER TO GO OUT ON SATURDAY. I — I WONDERED IF **WE** MIGHT DO THE SAME?
**WHAT?** OH, YEAH! THAT'D BE BRILLIANT. SEE YOU THEN.
WOW! EVERYTHING'S WORKED OUT RIGHT AFTER ALL! LOOKS LIKE IT'S **DONNA** WHO'S GOT NO CHANCE WITH GEOFF — NOT **ME!**
THE END

# OLD TIMERS

Whatever else you have in your wardrobe, these 10 items are well worth investing in. They'll never date — and they'll come in handy again and again.

## LITTLE BLACK DRESS

**L.B.D.**

L.B.D. means little black dress — something every girlie should have. Look for a simple style that won't date and you can haul it out every time a surprise party comes up and you don't want to have a big clothes crisis.

## SWEAT IT

A cosy sweat top will look great with jeans or dressed-up with chino style trousers. You can also team it with your sweat pants for a sporty look.

## LEG WORK

Leggings or sweat pants are another good investment. They'll make an all-go sporty outfit with a sweatshirt, trainers and denim jacket.

## JUST DENIM

The denim jacket's an old fave. You can throw it on anytime. Customise it with your favourite badges or patches, add studs or fringes — it's up to you!

## JEAN MACHINE

Levi 501's are expensive — but very classic. Look out for good quality jeans in the sales. Wear 'em with loafers or trainers and a nice thick belt.

## SMARTY PANTS

Smart trousers won't go amiss in your co-ordinated wardrobe. Add a top, a dress jacket and some loafers and you're ready for anything!

CLOTHES FROM C & A AND TOP SHOP ● SHOES FROM SAXONE

# OLD TIMERS

## GETTING SHIRTY

The ultimate versatile white shirt — it can be smart with a skirt and jacket, classy and casual with jeans or funky knotted over a black dress. Most people have one — and if you're anything like "Hi!'s" Fashion Ed, you'll have a whole selection!

## JACKET IN

The neat black jacket our model's wearing is good for a smart day-time look and doubles as a 'going out' jacket.

## LOVELY LOAFERS

You can get a good pair of chunky loafers from most shoe chain stores. The great thing about them is that they look good with jeans, smart with dressy trousers and great with a dress.

## FLIRTY SKIRTY

A simple skirt won't let you down when you need to look tidy and can be dressed up with a glam top and accessories for night time.

# ALBERT SQUARE

**Where's the best place to spend Christmas? At home in good old Britain or off Down Under? Our guide tells us what to expect from an EastEnders' Christmas or a Summer Bay one.**

**WEATHER:** We always hope we're going to get a white Christmas, but it never happens, does it? Nope, it'll be pouring rain as usual!
**WEATHERWISE:** *2 out of 10.*

**FOOD:** The usual Christmas dinner of turkey and all the trimmings (the veg from Pete's stall, of course). If you can't be bothered cooking it yourself Ian'll probably be selling pre-cooked packs from the caf. After all, he is always trying to make *more* money, isn't he? Or, alternatively, you could go round to Pauline's. She'll be feeding the five thousand (just like her old mum used to) and moaning about it as usual.
**SCOFF RATING:** *6 out of 10.*

**PREZZIES:** Unless you lurve woolly hat and glove sets, you're going to be severely disappointed. Pauline gets one every year, no doubt bought from Kath's stall. Pat's bound to find tacky earrings in her stocking and Sharon'll give Michelle some disgusting orange blusher.
**PRESENT PERFORMANCE:** *4 out of 10.*

**ENTERTAINMENT:** Just what do you do when it's raining cats and dogs, the shops are shut and it's James Bond or Indiana Jones on TV AGAIN? Argue with everyone else, of course! Yup, that age-old pastime of fighting with the family comes out tops every time. Well, everyone's bound to be sick of Pauline. Then, in the evening they can trot off to the Vic for a good old sing-song. Just think, clustered round the piano, Sharon 'singing' and Fat Pat in a spangly jumper and shocking pink eyeshadow. Great, eh?
**ENTERTAINMENT VALUE:** *3 out of 10 (or 10 out of 10 if you want a good laugh at their outfits!)*

**HUNK AVAILABILITY:** Who would you like to be caught under the mistletoe with? Well, there's Ian (yum), or, if you like the rough 'n' ready types, Grant and Phil Mitchell. Mind you, they're getting on a bit. Ricky does save the day, but all in all, Albert Square's a bit of a dead loss in the snogging department.
**KISSABILITY RATING:** *5 out of 10.*

**TOTAL:** *20 out of 50.*

# SUS Summer Bay

**WEATHER:** Absolutely no chance of a white Christmas here whatsoever, but it will be hot, hot, hot! Scorching sunshine's got to be better than rain any day.
**WEATHER WISE:** *9 out of 10.*

**FOOD:** You can have traditional Christmas dinner here, too, but you can all head to the beach and chuck your turkey on the barbecue. Alf will be in charge (wearing a chef's hat and plastic pinny) and Ailsa and Bobby'll be helping out.
**SCOFF RATING:** *8 out of 10.*

**PREZZIES:** Summer Bay kids'll get fun things for Crimbo like skateboards, surfboards and wild 'n' wacky t-shirts. No scarf and glove sets here, chums (except maybe for Celia!).
**PRESENT PERFORMANCE:** *8 out of 10.*

**ENTERTAINMENT:** After stuffing your face with turkey and Pavlova cake (everyone in Australia eats Pavlova) you can laze around in the sun for a while. Then you can play some beach volleyball, ride the surf (on your new board), or go for a trip on a boat. *Then,* it's party on into the night with pumpin' sounds provided by Lance and Martin.
**ENTERTAINMENT VALUE:** *10 out of 10.*

**HUNK AVAILABILITY:** Absolutely no shortage of hunks at all. Choose from Steven, Adam, Matt, lovely Mr Mitchell — the list is endless. You might not be quite so happy if you end up under the mistletoe with Lance, Martin or Mr Fisher, but all in all, it's lookin' good.
**KISSABILITY RATING:** *9 out of 10.*

**TOTAL:** *44 out of 50.*

**So there you have it — it's perfectly obvious we'd all rather be sunning ourselves in Summer Bay than going off down the 'knees-up'. Book the plane tickets now!**

Hi!
craig McLachlan

# too old!

**PART ONE**

GREAT! I SAW YOU IN THE LAST SCHOOL CONCERT. YOUR SOLO WAS BRILLIANT.
SO **THAT'S** HOW HE KNOWS MY NAME!
At lunchtime —
COMING TO THE WIMPY AFTER SCHOOL, LYNN?
I CAN'T, CHRIS. I-I'M GOING TO THE CAFE WITH TOM LEE.
YOU'RE WHAT? TOM LEE'S **FAR** TOO OLD FOR YOU!
COME ON! HE'S HARDLY **ANCIENT!** BESIDES, I FANCY HIM!
DON'T WE ALL! BUT I **STILL** THINK HE'S TOO OLD!
After school —
HI, LYNN — GLAD YOU COULD MAKE IT!
I CAN HARDLY BELIEVE THIS IS HAPPENING TO ME! TOM'S ABSOLUTELY FANTASTIC!
In the cafe —
HEY, THIS IS NICE!
YEAH! MY MATES AND I MEET UP HERE QUITE OFTEN. NOW, COME ON. TELL ME A BIT ABOUT YOURSELF!
Eventually —
THERE'S A REALLY GOOD FILM ON AT THE PLAZA TOMORROW. D'YOU WANT TO GO?
I'D LOVE TO, TOM.

**continued on page 54.**

# SHORTCUT TO...

**How many new year resolutions from 1991 did you succeed in keeping? Bet you can count 'em using no fingers! Well, here's our guide to help you — the hard way . . . and the easy way.**

### I resolve to stop fighting with my little bruv.

Next time you feel yourself about to lose your cool, count to ten and think about something ever so lurvely like that time he saved his pennies for three whole weeks 'cause he knew how much you wanted that classy CD player in Dixon's window. Okay — £1.50 doesn't go very far, but it's the thought that counts! Aawww!

**On the other hand, avoid ever feeling like losing your cool in the first place by keeping him bound and gagged in the cupboard under the stairs. Out of sight, out of mind — as the saying goes!**

### I resolve to do my homework straight after Neighbours.

Set your books out in front of you before you sit down to watch Neighbours. That way, there's no effort involved with having to get up and start when Neighbours finishes. Put the TV off when the credits come up at the end and get on with your homework at *once*! Remind yourself that it's only the news that's on so you're not missing anything. It's a whole hour before anything decent comes on TV, so make the time fly, by burying your head in a book or five!

**Mind you, good TV progs aren't honestly the only things stopping you doing your homework, are they? In fact, you'd probably rather watch a party political broadcast than do your algebra formulae. Don't despair — there *is* a way to keep this resolution. Watch Neighbours as usual, but set the old video recorder, too. Then at 10.00 pm when you *still* haven't opened a book, play back your Neighbours tape, *then* cram in your homework. There — you've done your stuff straight after Neighbours!**

### I resolve to stop crying buckets over my rat of an ex.

C'mon — think about the rotten things he did and said, the times you felt bored but didn't say, the times he felt bored and *did* say, the times he didn't phone, the times he didn't turn up for dates, the times he flirted with your mates . . . the list is endless. Write it down and read it every time you feel tempted to chase him. Would you honestly want this rat back? Is he worth the tears? If he was enough of a rat, you should realise you're better off without him. Look around at all those other guys and let them take your mind off the rat!

**Yeah, true enough — finding someone else is a solution . . . but the most important thing is to make sure it's one of your ex's swoonsome mates. This way, you kill two birds with one stone — you'll take your mind off the rat *and* get on his nerves at the same time. His ego will be somewhat dented when it's apparent you're getting on fine *without* him, and it'll be well and truly caved in when he realises it's his mate you're getting on fine *with*!**

### I resolve to stop nicking off with my sister's clothes.

Probably what bugs your sister most is you not *asking* before you 'borrow' her gear. And finding her new top, after an hour's search, in a crumpled heap (complete with coke stain) in the corner of your room probably doesn't go down too well either. Come to a compromise. Is there anything of *yours* she'd like to borrow in return? Get your mum to witness you promising to pay for any damage (this should reassure big sis!) — then be extra careful not to *do* any damage. Return your sister's clothes clean and ironed every time and who knows, she might even *force* her clothes on you — if only to get them back ironed!

**The secret here is not to actually stop nicking off with her clothes, but to stop being *caught*! Don't nick her gear when you're going to the same party, wait until she's chosen what she's going to wear that night, wait until she's left the house before donning her gear and make sure you get home first and dispose of the crumpled evidence in the bottom of *her* wardrobe. What she doesn't know won't hurt her . . . and *she* won't hurt *you* with a swift clip round the ear!**

### I resolve to do more exercise.

It's quite easy to do more exercise without working out in the gym for two hours every day. Make the most of P.E. at school and resist the temptation to 'forget' your kit. If there's a particular sport you enjoy, work towards getting in the school team. If this sounds too drastic a step so soon, then start off slowly by cutting out on buses, lifts from dad, lifts in shops etc. Walk or cycle from A to B whenever poss — and you'll eventually notice a difference.

**But why waste time walking up a flight of stairs when you can waste time waiting on the lift? Think of all those daily exercises you do without even realising — sleepwalking downstairs to the fridge every night, tapping your feet when you're waiting for the bus (or sometimes running to catch it!), tensing your muscles when Mum's in charge of driving you down town, walking round all those clothes racks on a Saturday, running round to get ready for the disco and as for all the hectic dancin' at the disco . . . phew! Huh — you couldn't fit in more exercise if you tried!**

### I resolve to stop getting steamed up over that 'cat' in 3c.

This catty girl certainly makes the steam come out of your ears, doesn't she? Well, next time she sniggers and sneers at someone's new hairdo, take a second look. Their hairstyle is brilliant compared to *hers*, isn't it? She's only trying to make herself feel better by putting other people down. So when she curls her lip at your new outfit, you can rest assured you're looking pretty darned trendy.

**Then again, it's not always that easy to shrug off her comments — they're non-stop and sooo unnecessary. Don't waste your dosh on a gag — this girl's mouth is too big. Instead, invest in a pair of fluffy ear-muffs — not to stop the steam coming out of your ears, but to give her good cause for comments . . . which *you* won't be able to hear!**

### I resolve to do a share of housework.

C'mon, think about it — how long does it take you to tidy your room or flee round the lounge with the hoover? Not long at all, eh? Think of your poor mum and all the *other* things she's got to do. What she wouldn't give to just have the hoovering and one bedroom to bother about. But if your bedroom tends to take a day to tidy then why not divide it up and tidy a little bit every night — wash those used plates, put your clothes in the laundry basket, *use* the waste paper bin, etc. Then when it comes to tidying your room at the end of the week, it'll just need a quick dusting.

**A share of the housework, eh? Well, you know how you always get the small 'half' when your brother shares a bar of choccie with you? This is how you should share the housework, too — share and share alike as they say. So when it's *your* turn to dust and *his* to hoover, swap! Let him finish the dusting (and put away the duster) before going to Mum and moaning that *you've* finished your dusting and *he* hasn't even started his hoovering. There, you've certainly given your brother a generous share.**

### I resolve to pay attention in class.

Come on, be honest — isn't it embarrassing every time the teacher hauls you up for talking or day-dreaming in class? There's only one thing to do . . . and that's to pay attention to what he or she is saying or writing on the blackboard. Wear blinkers (not literally) and keep your eyes directed firmly to the front of the classroom. Ignore your friend when she tries to get your attention. Just pretend you can't make out what she's whispering (half the time you really *can't*, anyway!) — save your gossiping for break-time, instead!

**Pay attention? In class? To what? Oh, to your chattering buddy two desks away . . . or those swoonsome fifth formers out there on the playing fields . . . or that mate who's passing a gossipy note your way . . . or that cute new guy in the front row. Pay attention in class? With pleasure!**

# SUCCESS

# the gree

## YOUR A

**We all know green's *the* colour to be, but do you really know how to go about it, or why you should bother? Read on!**

### ACID RAIN
Acid rain kills trees, poisons lakes and is caused by smoke from power stations and other industries dissolving in rain. The clouds containing it move around, so countries that are very guilty of producing it don't necessarily end up being too affected by it. Burning smokeless fuels and using less energy are two possible solutions.

### BUAV
In an ideal world all cosmetics would be cruelty-free, but sadly that just isn't the case. For details of companies whose products *are* animal friendly contact the BUAV (British Union for the Abolition of Vivisection) at 16a Crane Grove, Islington, London N7 8LB.

### CFCs
Used in fridges, some aerosols, and the plastic foam used to make fast food cartons, CFCs (chlorofluorocarbons to you!) are a major threat to the ozone layer — a fragile screen about 10-30 miles above the earth's surface. This filters out much of the sun's harmful ultra-violet rays — without it we'd all be baked alive — and yet we're still damaging and depleting it, putting ourselves in danger of contracting skin cancer and other diseases . . .

### DAMAGE
In the name of progress man has already caused untold damage to our environment — the consequences of which are only just beginning to be discovered.

### ENERGY
Conserving this is the name of the game! First of all it helps preserve our natural resources (they're being used up at a frightening rate!), secondly it reduces the amount of pollution being pumped into the atmosphere — thus not contributing to the greenhouse effect or acid rain problem — and lastly it saves money!

### FORESTS
Chopped down to provide grazing areas for cattle, paper for you to write on, (and so on!) forests take *years* to grow, yet only seconds to destroy! Not only do they look great and play host to a whole range of wildlife, they provide the invaluable service of converting carbon dioxide back into oxygen.

### GREENHOUSE EFFECT
Certain gases (eg. CFCs, methane, carbon dioxide) allow the sun's heat to penetrate the earth's atmosphere, but prevent it from escaping, and it is this which is known as the greenhouse effect. It's also known as 'Global Warming', which could eventually lead to vast areas of land disappearing under water forever. Why? Because if the earth begins to warm up the polar ice caps will start to melt. Oo-er!

### HOLIDAY
You just can't guarantee you'll end up sunbathing on golden sands and swimming in cool, clear water on holiday any more. Why? Because pollution caused by oil slicks and sewage have destroyed beaches here and all over the rest of the world.

### ILLNESS
Allergies, skin cancer, eye disease, food poisoning — they're all a sign that all is not well in our society and the sad thing is that the opposite should be true!

### JUICE
We're talking petrol, here! Vehicle exhausts are a major source of pollution and although using lead-free petrol helps, the only real solution is to encourage people to cycle and use public transport more often.

### KIND
This is what we all have to be to our planet in order to help it survive as long and as healthily as possible.

### LITTER
Litter is as serious a problem as any other on these pages. Products made

# a scene

## Z GUIDE!

from materials that aren't environmentally friendly can take years to decompose, (and some *never* will!) look awful, and endanger animal life. In severe states in cities, litter will also attract vermin and thus encourage the spread of disease.

### MASKS
Already a common sight in London, cyclists have been advised to wear masks to protect themselves from toxic exhaust fumes. Five or ten years ago who would ever have thought this would be completely acceptable?

### NOW
We've already taken too long to start helping our planet. If you haven't already started, you should do so *now,* as should your family, your friends, their families and so on.

### ORGANIC
Grown without the aid of man-made pesticides and fertilisers organic foods are the most natural you'll get. Grown for their taste (surely what food's about, after all!) rather than appearance, organic foods represent a return to nature in the best possible way.

### PLASTICS
Try to avoid plastics at all costs. *Making* them isn't environmentally friendly and neither is *using* them. Do your bit by refusing to accept excess plastic packaging and use your carrier bags till they burst. Plastics *never* disintegrate.

### QUESTIONS
If not enough is being done to help the environment in your area, demand to know why. Write to your local paper, the council, your MP and ask if schemes such as paper collection and bottle banks are available.

### RECYCLING
It makes sense — if we re-use paper, we won't need to chop down quite so many trees, etc. — and it doesn't take lots of time and effort on your part either. It's easy to think nothing *you* can do will help, but if everyone thought like that, nothing would *ever* happen. Organise a group of friends to collect bottles and paper, donate old clothes to charity instead of throwing them out, and find out who can make use of old stamps and empty cans.

### SPRAYS
Always stick to pump-action sprays because aerosols — even those which don't contain CFCs — can still contain *other* propellants which will pollute the atmosphere.

### TESTING
There are arguments for and against testing products on animals — some argue they're necessary in medical research, others that animals don't react to things in the same way as us so there's little point — but almost everyone agrees that testing cosmetics on animals is cruel and causes needless suffering.

### UNDERGROUND
Out of sight, out of mind, seems to be man's answer to certain problems, but burying toxic waste and other things underground is *not* the answer. It's just storing problems up for the future.

### VEGETARIANS
Scares over salmonella, listeria, BSE *and* a love of animals have led to lots of people following a vegetarian or even vegan diet. Previously considered a bit 'cranky', vegetarians are now accepted and fears for their health ("they won't get enough iron/protein") have proved totally groundless.

### WORRY
It's tempting to let all these facts 'n' figures worry you to death! But, as we've already said, there's plenty you *can* do, and the best way to put your mind at rest is to get yourself involved.

### EXTINCT
Hunting certain animals has already killed off entire species and left others struggling to survive. And, if people don't come to their senses, *more* animals are going to become extinct.

### YOUNG
This is who we must protect our planet for. *We're* all young ourselves, but we've got to enable generation after generation to enjoy their lives.

### ZOOS
It's a sad but true fact that zoos may soon be the only places we'll be able to see certain animals if we continue to ruin their habitat and endanger their lives.

# CRIMBO CROSSIE

**It's time to pit your wits against the biggest, baddest crossie around! No peeking at the answers, now!**

## ACROSS

1. You 11 Down under this plant (9)
6. Here, now, and gift-wrapped? (7)
8. Christmas trees and ozone friendly gifts are this (5)
9. Practical presents are ones you can --- (3)
12. Aladdin, Cinderella and Dick Whittington are these kind of characters (9)
13. --- turtle doves (3)
15. The kind of Christmas everyone dreams and sings about (5)
18. A spendable present (4)
20. Part of the 26 Down that go with turkey (8)
23. She sits at the top of your tree (5)
25. And 49 Across. Santa says this word in batches of three (2)
27. Every party has them (5)
28. The night before the big day (9, 3)
31. You can do this winter sport on 5 Down (3)
32. Food you 'gobble' up (6)
34. Hope it's one you like! (2)
37. A woman who's a man in panto (4)
38. A song sung at Christmas (5)
40. Something you can eat — or pull at Christmas (7)
42. And 45 Across. It follows Christmas Day(6, 3)
44. A famous reindeer's nose was this colour (3)
45. See 42 Across.
47. There are twelve days -- Christmas. (2)
49. See 25 Across (2)
50. Initials of the crumblie guy whose Christmas hit was "Merry Christmas, Everyone" (2)
52. Want to add something to your Christmas list? (2)
53. A precious metal carried by three wise men (4)
54. It's French for Christmas (4)
56. After this many nights decorations must come down (6)
57. We all eat too ---- over Christmas (4)
58. Some people start this in the middle of summer (8)

## ANSWERS

ACROSS:— 1. Mistletoe 6. Present 8. Green 9. Use 12. Pantomime 13. Two 15. White 18. Loot 20. Stuffing 23. Fairy 25. Ho 27. Games 28. Christmas Eve 31. Ski 32. Turkey 34. LP 37. Dame 38. Carol 40. Cracker 42. Boxing 44. Red 45. Day 47. Of 49. Ho 50. S.S. 52. P.S. 53. Gold 54. Noel 56. Twelve 57. Much 58. Shopping.

DOWN:— 1. Myrrh 2. Tinsel 3. Open 4. Tree 5. Snow 7. Eat 9. Up 10. Santa 11. Kiss 14. Winter 15. Wishbone 16. Icy 17. If 19. Of 21. Time 22. Frankincense 24. Yes 26. Trimmings 28. Carol 29. Sit 30. Ask 33. Yule Log 35. Partridge 36. Ice 38. Claus 39. Or 41. Rudolph 42. Buttons 43. Xmas 46. Party 48. Foil 51. Snap 52. Plan 55. Fun.

## DOWN

1. One of three gifts carried by three wise men (5)
2. It'll add colour to your tree! (6)
3. Bet you can't wait till your pressies are this! (4)
4. The evergreen item your pressies lie under (4)
5. Cold fluffy stuff you can make men from (4)
7. What you do, faced with loadsa luvverly grub (3)
9. Bet you get -- extra early on Christmas Day! (2)
10. And 38 down. The cuddly guy in a red suit and white beard (5, 5)
11. Do this under 1 Across (4)
14. The season everything on this page takes place in (6)
15. What you'll pull after Christmas dinner (8)
16. Weather to make you slip up! (3)
17. -- nobody liked you, you'd get zero presents and cards (2)
19. Wise men? There are three -- 'em (2)
21. At 3 p.m. it's ---- for the Queen's speech (4)
22. One of the gifts presented by the three wise men (12)
24. Will you say this to second helpings? (3)
26. Decorations or the bits 'n' pieces that go with your turkey (9)
28. Did you send one to everyone you knew . . . or not? (4)
29. This is all you'll want to do after eating your fill (3)
30. You'll have to pluck up courage to --- that hunk to the Crimbo Disco! (3)
33. It's traditionally burned at Christmas (4, 3)
35. Found in a pear tree, we believe (9)
36. A cold, hard skating surface (3)
38. See 10 Down (5)
39. It's French for 53 Across (2)
41. He was famous for his red nose (7)
42. Cinderella's (chocolate?) chum (7)
43. Christmas, in short (4)
46. An event at which you'll bop till you drop! (5)
48. Presents and turkey can get wrapped in this (4)
51. The noise your crackers should make (4)
52. If everything goes to ---- your Christmas should be merry (4)
55. What Christmas is all about (3)

# GUILTY!

JACKIE was always game for a laugh.
HOI, TRICIA — WHERE'D YOU GET THAT TOP YOU WERE WEARING ON SATURDAY? OXFAM?
VERY FUNNY, I **DON'T** THINK! GET LOST, JACKIE.
HEY, DON'T BE SO TOUCHY, TRICIA. I'VE GOT ONE THE SAME — I **KNOW** IT'S FROM SNOB.
OH, YOU KNOW TRICIA, JACKIE. NO SENSE OF HUMOUR. I DON'T KNOW WHY YOU BOTHER PULLING HER LEG.
I GUESS SO. SHE AND EMMA MUST BE THE TWO MOST BORING GIRLS IN THE SCHOOL. D'YOU RECKON THEY LAUGH AT **ANYTHING**?
I DOUBT IT. THEIR FACES WOULD CRACK UNDER THE STRAIN.

Then in Class —
THIS IS JENNI, EVERYONE. SHE'S JOINED OUR SCHOOL TODAY. I HOPE YOU'LL ALL MAKE HER FEEL WELCOME.
HI, JENNI! I'M JACKIE AND THIS IS DAWN. COME AND SIT WITH US.
OH, ER, THANKS!
SOME OF THE CLASS CAN BE A BIT IFFY BUT YOU'LL SOON GET TO KNOW EVERYONE.
DO WE GET MR HANSON FOR MANY LESSONS?
NO. HE'S JUST OUR REG TEACHER. WE SEE HIM TWICE A DAY — THAT'S ALL.
Later —
DON'T FORGET YOUR SWIMMING KIT FOR TOMORROW AFTERNOON OR MISS PHILIPS WON'T BE TOO AMUSED, JENNI.
OH, NO! I HATE SWIMMING. I'M HOPELESS AT IT. ANY IDEAS HOW TO GET OUT OF IT?
NONE AT ALL! YOU WON'T GET ROUND MISS PHILIPS WITH DAFT EXCUSES. ANYWAY, IT'S FUN!
THAT'S EASY FOR YOU TO SAY. BUT I DON'T SWIM TOO WELL.
DON'T WORRY! I'M A QUALIFIED LIFE SAVER. IF YOU SINK, I'LL SAVE YOU.
RIGHT, YOU TWO — I'M OFF TO CATCH MY BUS. SEE YOU TOMORROW.
Next morning —
JENNI WAS DEAD TOUCHY YESTERDAY ABOUT THE SWIMMING. D'YOU RECKON SHE CAN'T SWIM AT ALL?
HMM — MAYBE. BEST LAY OFF THE SUBJECT, JACKIE. I MEAN, SHE'LL FEEL A RIGHT NERD IF SHE'S THE ONLY NON-SWIMMER IN THE CLASS.

Later —
ER, JACKIE, CAN I HAVE A WORD, PLEASE?
SURE, MR HANSON — WHAT'S UP?
I'VE HAD A COMPLAINT FROM JENNI. SHE SAYS YOU'VE BEEN PICKING ON HER.
PICKING ON HER? **ME?**
YES, YOU! SHE SAYS YOU MADE HER LOOK FOOLISH OVER SWIMMING.
WE HAD A BIT OF A LAUGH, SIR, BUT THAT'S ALL. ONLY SOME JOKING — SAME AS ALWAYS.
MAYBE SHE'S JUST MISUNDERSTOOD. YOU **DO** GET CARRIED AWAY SOMETIMES!
I KNOW, SIR, BUT I EXPECT TO HAVE MY LEG PULLED BACK. IT WAS JUST A JOKE, HONEST!
I KNOW THAT — BUT DOES JENNI? JUST BE A BIT MORE CAREFUL IN FUTURE. OKAY?
OKAY!
At break —
IMAGINE GOING TO MR HANSON LIKE THAT — AND AFTER ALL YOU'VE DONE TO MAKE HER FEEL WELCOME. YOU DIDN'T TEASE HER ANY MORE AFTER I'D GONE FOR MY BUS, DID YOU?
OH, DON'T **YOU** START TOO, DAWN. HONESTLY, I DIDN'T DO **ANYTHING!**

AND THE MORE I THINK ABOUT IT, THE MADDER I GET. I'M GONNA SEE JENNI ABOUT THIS!
HANG ON, JACK. IF SHE'S FEELING A BIT FUNNY SHE COULD READ **ANYTHING** INTO WHAT YOU SAY. I THINK WE'D BEST AVOID HER FOR THE TIME BEING.
HMM! MAYBE YOU'RE RIGHT. WHERE IS SHE ANYWAY?
IN CLASS — WHERE **WE** SHOULD BE. COME ON!
At break —
LOOKS LIKE JENNI'S CHUMMED UP WITH TRICIA AND EMMA. WELL, THAT EXPLAINS EVERYTHING.
EH? HOW D'YOU MEAN?
IT'S SIMPLE. IF JENNI LIKES **THEIR** COMPANY SHE OBVIOUSLY DOESN'T HAVE A SENSE OF HUMOUR, EITHER.
YOU'RE RIGHT, EINSTEIN. WE'RE BETTER OFF WITHOUT HER.
But a week later —
I WARNED YOU LAST WEEK ABOUT YOUR BEHAVIOUR, JACKIE — BUT IT SEEMS YOU TOOK NO NOTICE. JENNI'S **STILL** GETTING A HARD TIME FROM YOU NEARLY EVERY DAY.
WHAT?
SHE'S VERY UPSET, JACKIE. AND TRICIA AND EMMA HAVE BEEN IN HERE EVERY TIME TO BACK HER UP, SO THERE'S NO POINT IN DENYING IT.
BUT, SIR — I HAVEN'T EVEN SPOKEN TO JENNI ALL WEEK! HONESTLY, MR HANSON.
DON'T LIE TO ME, JACKIE. JUST STOP PICKING ON JENNI OR I'LL HAVE TO TAKE THIS MATTER FURTHER.
WHAT ON EARTH IS THIS? WHAT'S GOING ON?

Jackie spoke to Dawn —
HONESTLY, DAWN, I'M GOBSMACKED. MR HANSON GOT QUITE SHIRTY WITH ME. HE SAID TRICIA AND EMMA WENT IN AND BACKED JENNI UP.
I WOULDN'T PUT ANYTHING PAST THOSE TWO. THEY LOVE STIRRING.
I'M GONNA HAVE TO GET TO THE BOTTOM OF THIS. I CAN'T BE ACCUSED OF BULLYING SOMEONE WHEN I HAVEN'T EVEN SPOKEN TO THEM.
BE CAREFUL, JACKIE. YOU COULD MAKE THINGS WORSE.
HOW, DAWN? I'VE BEEN WRONGFULLY ACCUSED OF SOMETHING SO I'VE A RIGHT TO KNOW WHAT'S GOING ON.
So —
WHAT'S ALL THIS ABOUT ME BULLYING YOU, JENNI? YOU KNOW I HAVEN'T DONE ANYTHING OF THE SORT.
WHAT? OH, ER, JACKIE!
HEY! LEAVE JENNI ALONE, YOU BULLY.
WHO RATTLED YOUR CAGE, TRICIA JONES? THIS IS BETWEEN JENNI AND ME.
OH, YEAH? WELL WE DON'T LIKE BULLIES, DO WE, EMMA? WE THINK THEY SHOULD BE HAULED UP BEFORE THE HEAD AND MADE TO LOOK THE CREEPS THEY ARE.
NOW HANG ABOUT. I'M NOT THE ONE WHO'S A BULLY.

TELL THEM, JENNI. I'VE NEVER BULLIED YOU IN MY LIFE.
LEAVE ME ALONE, JACKIE. JUST GO AWAY.
NO, I WON'T. I WANT . . .
JACKIE, LOOK OUT!
JACKIE! OBVIOUSLY YOU STILL HAVEN'T TAKEN ANY NOTICE OF ANYTHING I'VE SAID.
OH, MR HANSON. IT'S NOT WHAT YOU THINK . . .
ISN'T IT? COME WITH ME, JACKIE. YOU'RE GOING TO SEE THE HEAD.
BULLYING IS A VERY SERIOUS OFFENCE, JACKIE. AND MR HANSON HAD JUST SAID HE CAUGHT YOU RED-HANDED.
BUT IT ISN'T TRUE, MRS MCKAY. I WAS ONLY TRYING TO GET TO THE TRUTH. I'VE BEEN SET UP!
BUT WHY, JACKIE? WHY SHOULD JENNI GO TO MR HANSON NEARLY EVERY DAY IN TEARS ABOUT YOU?
I DON'T KNOW, MRS MCKAY. BUT ASK MY MATE, DAWN. SHE'LL TELL YOU I HAVEN'T BEEN NEAR JENNI.

I'M SURE WE WILL SEE DAWN, TOO, JACKIE. BUT MEANWHILE I HAVE NO ALTERNATIVE BUT TO SUSPEND YOU.
B-BUT I'LL MISS LOADS OF CLASSWORK . . .
TOTTENHAM HOTSPUR
That evening —
WHAT AM I GONNA DO, DAWN? NO ONE BELIEVES ME . . . NOT EVEN MUM AND DAD. IT'S JUST MY WORD AGAINST JENNI'S.
DON'T WORRY, JACKIE. I THINK I'M ON TO SOMETHING, BUT I WON'T SAY TILL I'M SURE.
The next day —
WHAT ARE YOU WRITING, JENNI?
GO AWAY. IT'S PRIVATE.
YOUR PLANS HAVE GONE UP THE CREEK, HAVEN'T THEY? NOW JACKIE'S BEEN SUSPENDED, YOU CAN'T GO SNIVELLING TO MR HANSON AT EVERY CHANCE.
WHAT D'YOU MEAN? ARE YOU GOING TO BULLY ME, TOO?
NO, I'M JUST HELPING MY MATE OUT. LET'S TAKE A LOOK AT THIS.
NO! LEAVE IT ALONE.
WELL, WELL! JUST AS I THOUGHT. MR HANSON'S NAME IN A HEART. YOU'VE GOT A CRUSH ON HIM, HAVEN'T YOU?
SO?

SO MY MATE'S IN BIG TROUBLE BECAUSE OF YOU. YOU KNOW SHE HASN'T BEEN BULLYING YOU. YOU JUST WANTED AN EXCUSE TO GO AND SEE MR HANSON, DIDN'T YOU? SO YOU COULD GET HIS ATTENTION.
YOU WON'T TELL, WILL YOU?
I WON'T. BUT **YOU'RE** GOING TO. YOU'RE NOT THE FIRST GIRL TO HAVE A CRUSH ON HIM AND YOU WON'T BE THE LAST.
CAN I HAVE MY PAPER BACK?
YEAH! AFTER YOU'VE SEEN MR HANSON AND SORTED ALL THIS OUT.
Jenni had no choice, and —
PROPER LITTLE SHERLOCK HOLMES, AREN'T YOU, DAWN? WHAT PUT YOU ON TO THE SCENT?
JUST THE WAY SHE KEPT LOOKING AT MR HANSON, THAT'S ALL. AFTER ALL, I HAD A MASSIVE CRUSH ON HIM LAST YEAR, REMEMBER.
AND TRICIA AND EMMA WERE JUST OUT TO STIR THINGS. JENNI KNEW THEY DIDN'T LIKE YOU SO SHE KNEW THEY'D BACK HER. THEY'RE IN MORE TROUBLE THAN SHE IS.
YOU'RE TERRIFIC, DAWN. I THINK I'LL AWARD YOU THE GRAND ORDER OF THE STRAW HAT.
EH? WHY?
'COS YOU'RE GETTING MORE LIKE MISS MARPLE BY THE MINUTE.


**THE END**

# WELL *cringeworthy!*

**Do your mum and big sis groan every time the stylus drops on to your fave album? And do they sneer and giggle at your pin-ups . . . and ask what on earth they're wearing on Top Of The Pops? Well, prepare yourself for an eyeful of what *they* idolised!**

Surprise! Surprise! It's Cilla 'ere! Yep, *she* was the Kylie of the sixties, with many hits including "Anyone Who Had A Heart" — get singin', Mum! Cop an eyeful of that eyeshadow — worra mess! Cilla led the way in black eyeliner, false eyelashes, glitzy shifts and horrific vinyl boots. Yeuch! Mind you, the threads she wears on Blind Date haven't improved much — though her nose has. She's had a nose job since her chart-topping heyday, y'see.

Wow! Check out those flares! And crumblies have the nerve to laugh at The Stone Roses. These lads were The Bay City Rollers and they were *mega* with hits like "Shang-a-lang" and "Bye-bye, Baby". And the *hair* on these guys — talk about Frankenstein features! By now, the oldies in your house should be blushing furiously at the thought of those hideous platform shoes and bell bottom trews that they used to wear with pride. The Bay City Rollers were also heavily into tartan scarves, waistcoats, trims and insets on their flares — and so were their fans! Imagine having *that* little lot lurking in *your* wardrobe.

Well, lookee here — betcha don't recognise the mega star in this pic at the start of his career with The Jackson Five (there's a clue for you!).

Yep, that's Michael Jackson there in the middle wearing a rather fetching green jacket with shiny Concorde wing collared shirt. Then there's the reverse print trousers with contrasting inset for added flare. Can you believe it? And here's a piccie of Michael nowadays just to show how his looks have changed thanks to a new wardrobe . . . and a new face! Hmm! But have they changed for the better?



C

Toyah Wilcox is better known nowadays as the one in the Mum deodorant ad. She's into acting quite a bit these days. But at the end of the seventies, beginning of the eighties, she was a shocking songster — a birrova Madonna of the time, with weird and wonderful clothes, jewellery, lyrics and hairstyles (and hair colours). Your big sis will remember Toyah numbers like "It's A Mystery" and "Thunder In The Mountains" — sung with a lithp — oops, sorry, lisp. Don't let your big sis take the mickey out of Madonna again . . . and don't let your sister tell you she never admired Toyah with her 'unusual' looks. Luckily, Toyah's more down-to-earth these days and her hair hasn't fallen out with all that back-combing and dye.

Believe it or not, Duran Duran were once the equivalent of New Kids where mass hysteria was concerned. Here's how they looked when they made their debut with "Planet Earth". And here's how they look now with only three of the original members. In the old piccie that's John Taylor on the left, Simon standing at the back and Nick Rhodes sitting in the middle. In the newer piccie Nick's on the left with cropped bleached hair. Yeuch! When your sis sneers and laughs at the way you go overboard with 'lurve' for the New Kids, just ask her if the reason she doesn't like New Kids is because they don't wear headscarves, frilly shirts, jackets with collars up, suede 'Robin Hood' boots and a ton of make-up. Ha, ha!

Remember Adam Ant's single, "Room At The Top"? It didn't even get *near* to topping the charts. But in the *eighties*, Adam and the Ants raced up the charts with hits like "Stand and Deliver". Ant fever was rife! Adam Ant was *the* swashbuckling swoonsome hunk of the early eighties — at least in the eyes of Liz and the TV Ed. He had braided plaits of hair here and there, black eyeliner, belts, buckles, scarves and feathers — and we mustn't forget the famous stripe of white make-up across his face! We're not going to take the mickey out of Adam's early eighties image because we reckon he was much hunkier then than now.

And here's someone else your big sis will have fond memories of — Boy George in his Culture Club days. They had lotsa chart toppers like "Do You Really Want To Hurt Me" and "Karma Chameleon". But check the make-up. Did we say *Duran Duran* wore a ton of the stuff? Never again will your sis be able to bug you rotten with her hyena impersonation when she sees Adamski in *his* clobber.

P.S. We couldn't resist putting in *this* late seventies pic of someone else you all know. Yes, conclusive proof that even Hi!'s trendiest letter opener had her cringeworthy moments in fashion. Check that gipsy dress and the feather haircut!

And here's the wackiest lady we have around at the mo — pretty tame after Toyah and Boy George. Just think on this, though — your mum was black affronted at that piccie of Cilla and some day *you'll* be black affronted at the sight of Madonna, Adamski, New Kids, Kylie, The Stone Roses or Poison. Then again, maybe you already feel like that!

# Starry-Eyed

**Forget those swoonsome dreams in which cutie Kristian Schmid buys you a red rose for every minute of the day. He's about as romantic as a dose of liver salts . . . as we found out when we asked him and a few of your other fave peeps about their most romantic Crimbo offerings!**

### KRISTIAN SCHMID

. . . RECEIVED

I've been given the usual kind of romantic presents — teddy bears and stuff, love hearts, y'know. But that's about it, I'm afraid. Sniff!

. . . GAVE

Erm . . . no, I'm not gonna give you a very good answer here, either. I don't know, erm . . . nope, I can't think of anything — sorry. I'm not really romantic, y'see.

### LINDA HARTLEY

. . . RECEIVED

Most romantic Christmas present I've ever received? That's tricky — I get so many romantic gifts from John, my husband, y'see. One Christmas he bought me a gorgeous ring made by an Australian jeweller who bases his designs on Egyptian hieroglyphics. The design on my ring is called Lady of Heaven — John says I'm *his* Lady of Heaven, y'see. (Blush.)

. . . GAVE

The most romantic Christmas present I've *bought* would be the time I gave John a bottle of Champagne, a bouquet of flowers and an emerald earring! (Hmm!? — The Ed).

### MOUCHE PHILLIPS

. . . RECEIVED

Romantic? Oh, er, I don't think I've ever received anything very romantic. Erm, I've been sent romantic poems and cards from a boy, once. And flowers y'know — nothing really original.

. . . GAVE

And I can't think of any romantic presents I've given someone. Sorry!

### TREV AND SIMON

. . . RECEIVED

Trev: The most romantic Christmas present I've ever received was a Tom and Jerry calendar about two inches square. It's hanging up on the bathroom door! (Hmm? again! — The Ed).

. . . GAVE

I've bought salt 'n' pepper sets from the 50 pence shop for Christmas presents! Would you like one? (No thanks — The Ed). But I've also bought some clothes for my girlfriend's Christmas.

. . . RECEIVED

Simon: Most romantic Chrissie pressie? I was once given a cup and saucer set with a Matisse design. The cup was silver so that the picture on the saucer reflected on it.

. . . GAVE

And I once gave my girlfriend a wooden circus set from Paris. It had loads of little animals, and it was a puzzle, too!

## TONY GREGORY

. . . RECEIVED

Oh, wow, that's a really difficult question. I mean, I dunno — what's a romantic present? I can't think of anything particularly romantic I've received. Usually, I just get given fun things for a laugh, y'know.

. . . GAVE

And the most romantic present I've ever given? This is a horrible question . . . the same thing goes really. I can't think of anything. I mean, there's the usual rubbish like a box of chocolates and a nice bottle of wine and all that stuff but I tend to give really daft and stupid presents to take the mickey. None of them are romantic.

## ANDY CRANE

. . . RECEIVED

I don't think I've ever been bought anything that can be described as classically romantic. I got a leather jacket once for Christmas from a girlfriend. And Yvette would buy me things she knew I liked, which you wouldn't class as romantic — nice jumpers and sort of, y'know . . . well, I don't worry about what it is they buy me — it's who buys it for me that I'm bothered about.

. . . GAVE

As a Christmas present, I bought Yvette a weekend in Paris. But I didn't actually get round to taking her until April. I furiously maintained that it was supposed to be Paris in the Spring — but she says that really I just never got round to doing it till then. So I suppose that's a fairly romantic thing to do. So all she actually got for Christmas was a travel brochure of Paris. But it was like the Generation Game and she said, "Oh, you've bought me a travel brochure," then she opened it up and inside were the tickets. Aw!

## LIZ

. . . RECEIVED

Me? Huh! I've never received a romantic present! Oh, no, you're not writing this down for everyone to see, are you? Well, let me think, then . . . the only thing a certain ex ever bought for me was Duncan, my first hamster. Sniff!

. . . GAVE

I don't buy romantic presents — I buy fun things. I once sent someone a red rose, though — which had the desired effect, shall we say? And I've sent Tom Cruise a romantic poem for Christmas . . . and for Valentine's Day and for his birthday . . . and for the Queen's two birthdays . . .

## DANIELLA WESTBROOK

. . . RECEIVED

Erm, last year I got an eternity bracelet from my boyfriend — it's a gold bangle like a slave bracelet, y'know. It's lovely. Bless him. Sigh!

. . . GAVE

Let me think . . . I *am* romantic but I usually tend to buy silly cards and presents for a laugh. I haven't bought anyone anything romantic but . . . maybe this year, I'll think of something romantic . . .

## NEIL BUCHANAN

. . . RECEIVED

The most romantic Christmas present I've ever been given? Hmm — I can't think of anything here . . . 'cos I suppose it's not necessarily the object that's romantic — it's the thought behind it, and the effort. In other words, erm, I can't think of anything here.

. . . GAVE

The most romantic Christmas present I have ever *given* someone though, was . . . erm, I was going out with this girl and I was really in love with her and we couldn't spend Christmas day together — I had my Christmas present for her wrapped up and on Christmas morning I woke up and I was so unhappy 'cos I wasn't with her that I went and wrote a song. It just all came rolling out and I just poured it into a tape and then I wrapped it up with her present and she cried when she got it. And actually, that song was on the first album I did when I was in a rock band, Marseilles, many moons ago.

# 1992 AND ALL

**We're joining the European Open Market, trade barriers are coming down . . . in fact, all sorts of barriers will be coming down, so we thought we'd help you suss out our neighbours (the male ones) so you'd be ready. Here's our fun guide to European guys!**

## GERMANY

### APPEARANCE

Tall and big, with blond hair and blue eyes, that's your larger-than-life German — who's only really grown so tall and strong because he eats everything in sight! Don't leave anything even remotely edible lying around when there's a German nearby — our TV Ed says they're like locusts! (She once went very hungry when she sat at a table with several hungry Germans, looked away for a few seconds, and found there was no food left when she looked back!) Style-wise, you'd be better going out with a Brit! Germans tend to favour loud 'golfing' jumpers, clumpy boots and very severe haircuts. Yummy we *don't* think!

### WHERE YOU'LL FIND HIM

Being sporty, swotty or piggy! Check out tennis courts, libraries and nosh-houses and you'll quickly find your German. You'll need to be fit to keep up with him, though!

### HOW TO IMPRESS HIM

Challenge him to an eating competition and win! (Tip: starve for *months* beforehand.) Tell him the ins and outs of each British political party since the year dot . . . he'd be stunned into silence. (Pleading total ignorance is easier.)

### WHY YOU SHOULD BOTHER

They make good sausages, but you'll have a fight to get near them!

## FRANCE

### APPEARANCE

Everyone, but everyone, knows that French peeps are stylish. True? False! Some of them are, in fact *lots* of them are . . . oh, all right then, *heaps* of them are, but the Beauty Ed remembers having the most unfashionable French student *ever* at her school and the Pop Ed can vouch for the fact that there were more than a few fashion victims trotting around the last time *she* was in the land of baguettes, so don't get too downhearted! Most French lads *are* stunningly stylish and gorgeous but there are still a *few* amongst them who haven't yet figured out that sea, sand and socks just don't go!

### WHERE YOU'LL FIND HIM

Lounging around almost anywhere! Cafes, beaches, arty cinemas, you name it — he'll be sussing you out from behind his shades. What he'll *never* do, though, is participate in anything sporty — getting hot 'n' sweaty is not his scene.

### HOW TO IMPRESS HIM

Beat him in the style stakes, never take off your shades and practise your French till it's perfect!

### WHY YOU SHOULD BOTHER

Um . . . Paris in the springtime's supposed to be luvverly, the French bake better bread than us and well . . . we suppose we should learn to love our new neighbours!

# THAT . . .

## ITALY

In a style-trial, these swanky chaps'd turn up trumps — and *no* mistake! There's not much you can teach any Italian about how to look good and dress well, all of which can end up giving *you* quite an inferiority complex. Dark haired and a scrummy bronzed brown, with a perfect set of gleaming white gnashers, Italians are utterly lovely lads! You won't find *them* in socks and sandals on yer beach!

### WHERE YOU'LL FIND HIM

Hanging out in cafes, drinking Coke and cappuccino — in fact, being a bit of a lounge lizard almost anywhere. When the going gets hot, Italians stay cool . . .

### HOW TO IMPRESS HIM

Ignoring him would work wonders if you could possibly manage to do it . . . he then wouldn't be able to resist the challenge of trying to impress *you!* However, if that doesn't work (and let's face it, it'd be hard!), you should praise his mama's pasta — but don't scoff too much unless you want to grow up to be like her.

### WHY YOU SHOULD BOTHER

Are you kidding? He's gorgeousness on legs and not to be missed!

## BELGIUM

It's sad, but true. No one in the entire "Hi!" office has ever met a Belgian or knows anyone who has. We're sure they're incredibly lovely lads, though, and if any of them would like to invite us over — just to make sure — we'll gladly accept and will certainly include them in future features. Honest injun!

## SWITZERLAND

Swiss lads are very like German lads 'cept they're skinnier, not nearly so greedy and they yodel more! (Yup! None of us has met a Swiss lad either, but again, we'd be happy to if the offer arose!)

## SPAIN

### APPEARANCE

Small, hairy and greasy, that's your average Spaniard, we're afraid. (Well, so the Ed says anyway, and who are we to mess with her!) It's a strong possibility that medallion men originated in Spain because Spaniards don't seem to feel happy wearing anything unless it's accompanied by lotsa gold — the more chunky rings and chains, the better! Still, at least they're brown. (An unfortunate thing about Spain is 'orrible British blokes seem to lurve it, but they're easy to spot and avoid. Pink people in Union Jack shorts are *not* Spanish okay?)

### WHERE YOU'LL FIND HIM

Scurrying around beaches, pools, cafes, streets . . . you name it, he'll be there! In fact, even in places you don't want to find him, you probably will . . .

### HOW TO IMPRESS HIM

Grin and nod a lot.

### WHY YOU SHOULD BOTHER

Um . . . pass!

## DENMARK

### APPEARANCE

They're not called great Danes (har har) for nowt, these lads. Tall, lean and luvverly, they're yet another sporty people, who can usually be seen bounding around at all times of the day and night in terribly trendy sporty stuff . . . and not just for effect! Be warned. If you want to keep up with a Dane, you've gotta be prepared to invest in loadsa pairsa trainers! *And* not mind them never steppin' out of their sporting gear. (Pooh!)

### WHERE YOU'LL FIND HIM

Resting in his room, looking up sporty books in the library so that he knows *everything* about his chosen sport, or pursuing excellence in his chosen field, pool, gym . . . you name it!

### HOW TO IMPRESS HIM

Search us! You could walk around with your hair dyed bright blue and he wouldn't be impressed unless you could equal his crawl, jog or tennis stroke. (Mind you, dyeing your hair bright blue wouldn't get you anywhere with anyone else either!)

### WHY YOU SHOULD BOTHER

He speaks English nicely and your gran would definitely approve!

## NETHERLANDS

### APPEARANCE

Pretty darned hunky, if their appearance in the World Cup is anything to go on — although you could be forgiven for thinking they're all dark-skinned with dreadlocks! Very athletic, most of them are tall and fair with strong muscly legs — it's all that cycling around flat old Holland, you see! Style-wise, they're more of the jeans 'n' jumpers brigade, but their hunky good looks make them more of a catch than quite a few others on this page.

### WHERE YOU'LL FIND HIM

Tending tulips? Actually Dutch blokes are pretty much like British blokes — apart from their accents — and *especially* when it comes to footie. Get out and about on yer bike, too!

### HOW TO IMPRESS HIM

Swot up on footie, flaunt your bike — but remember he's one of the few people in the world who won't *need* or be that impressed by a "mountain" bike (ho, ho) — oh, and learn a few words of Dutch. Peasy!

### WHY YOU SHOULD BOTHER

Flowers, cycling and Dutch lads are all plain *nice!*

## GREECE

### APPEARANCE

Cute, cuddly and bronzed, Greek lads aren't the most exciting dressers, but they don't make that many mistakes either. (Probably because all you'll see them in is shorts, trunks and T-shirt). Unlike Spaniards, they're not hot on jewellery (whew!), but their colouring *is* similar, and pretty nice, too! Oh, they also have extra-long eyelashes to flutter at you! (Swoon!)

### WHERE TO FIND HIM

Anywhere and everywhere! Discos, the beach, markets, your pool, he'll be there!

### HOW TO IMPRESS HIM

By being friendly and attentive, you'll impress him so much that he'll want you to meet every member of his family and name all his children after you . . . Greeks need very little encouragement.

### WHY YOU SHOULD BOTHER

The food's good, the weather's fine and a few free hols never go amiss!

# HAIR RA

**It's party time again and you've got to look fab 'n' funky without spending a lot of dosh. Well, never fear, we are here (!), with happenin' hairstyles for practically nought pence.**
**We used coloured pipecleaners and raffia to liven up the styles, and you can easily obtain them from your local arty-crafty supplies shop.**

**1.** Try this style if you've got shoulder length or shorter curly or thick hair. Simply divide your hair into sections and wind pipecleaners round at the roots, so that the sections stand up. What could be easier? It's wild.

# SING!

**3.** To do this you'll have to sit for ages first and cut your raffia into short strips. Then sit for another half hour or so folding them in half and attaching them to kirby grips. Now pile your hair up loosely and keep it firmly in place using all your grips. Gently pull the raffia, so that it stands up.

**2.** This is easy peasy lemon-squeezy and works on straight or curly hair. Simply put your hair up into a pony tail and tie some lengths of raffia around it. Now make spiral curls by winding sections of hair round curling tongs. Wind from the roots first, wrapping your hair round the barrel of the tongs. Curl the raffia in the same way- don't worry it won't burn or melt (we hope!!) -et voila!
If you've got shorter hair you can attach the raffia curls with kirby grips.

**4.** This one's a bit more complicated and you may need someone to give you a hand. We wove the hair from one side to another, but it works just as well woven down the back. Start off with one section like you would for a French plait and wind a pipe cleaner round it. Take more hair in from the sides and divide into two. Wind a pipecleaner round each section. Join the two together again and wind a pipecleaner round the whole thing. Repeat this taking in new sections of hair from the side every time you divide into two. Keep going until you reach the end and finish off with a few pipecleaners.

***Turn to page 114 for some movin' make-up ideas.***

# HOM
# CHR

# E FOR STMAS

"YOU wanted to see me?" Tina asked, as she pushed her way through to the corner table. It was Christmas Eve, and the little cafe was full of frazzled shoppers.

Lee looked up and smiled in the way she'd come to recognise. But there was a look on his face, a hesitancy that she'd never seen before.

"Hang on. You haven't got a drink."

He got to his feet and elbowed his way to the counter, coming back a few minutes later with a coke for her, and a refill for himself. Without asking, he'd bought a couple of mince pies — the sort she liked.

"Remember the first time we came here?" said Tina. "Just after Richard moved away."

"Yes," he nodded, as his long fingers played absent-mindedly with the holly-sprigged tablecloth. "I had to buy you two cokes to calm you down!"

Tina nodded, feeling her face flush as she looked away. She sighed, her thoughts going back to the day she'd stood waiting for Lee, outside school . . .

"Have — have you heard from Richard, yet, Lee?" she'd burst out, worried and embarrassed. "Only it's been two weeks now since his family left town, and . . ."

"And Richard's not too great at letter writing — as he probably told you before he went," Lee had said.

Then they fell into step and headed for the nearby cafe, and he'd said, "I remember when we were about twelve, he went abroad with his folks. I waited every day for a card with a Spanish stamp."

"And he brought it home with him, 'cos he forgot to post it! I know, he told me!"

Over the months they'd been going out, Richard had told her quite a lot about his best mate, Lee. Tina felt as if she knew all about him already, and told him so.

"I feel like that, too — Richard's driven me mad! Tina this and Tina that!" Lee had replied, pushing a hand through the auburn hair that was so different to Richard's spiky blond locks. "He was really down in the dumps when his dad got that job — said he couldn't bear the thought of being a hundred miles away from you!"

"You okay, Tina?" Lee's voice cut into her thoughts, bringing her back to the present and the noisy, steam-filled cafe.

She blinked up at him, and smiled.

"Fine!" she said. "I — I just can't believe Richard's actually coming home again today!"

Her heart beat faster as she thought of the plans, made so long ago, and how the time had dragged until, at last, it was Christmas Eve!

For some reason Lee looked away, the tension returning to his face. Tina sighed, remembering how in those early, loneliest weeks it had been comforting to know she wasn't the only one missing Richard.

"We used to have a real laugh when we were in the juniors together," Lee would say, wistfully, trying to make her giggle by telling her some prank he and Richard got up to.

Missing Richard drew them into meeting regularly for a coke after school, or a walk in the park. Their early conversations all revolving around Richard. How one or the other had phoned him at his new home, and how he was saving the fare to come home for a weekend to stay with his gran.

"I — I thought I'd better come and let you know he's on his way!" Tina gabbled that night, almost two months ago, when she found herself on Lee's doorstep with a precious letter in her hand. "I know he'll want to see you — he was really grateful when I told him you've been looking after me!"

As she looked up at Lee, leading her smiling into his house, she'd felt warm and comfortable — glad to be sharing the news of Richard's planned first visit.

Now Tina drank her coke, only half aware that Lee had begun to say something. She thought of that weekend and how, though Richard *said* nothing had changed, there had been a restlessness about him. It almost made her feel she didn't know him any more.

But that had been before she rang him and got the news that all the family were coming home for Christmas — actually on Christmas Eve — to spend some time with his gran!

"It's going to be great, Lee!" she said, across the cafe table, putting her excited thoughts into words. "We'll have loads of news from school for him, and there's so much planned for Christmas!"

"I-I'm really sorry, Tina!"

Startled, Tina stared as Lee mumbled the totally unexpected words.

His face white, his concerned blue eyes avoiding hers, he pulled a crumpled letter out of his pocket.

"I got this from Richard — to say there's been a change of plan," he said, sheepishly. "His mum's not well, so the rest of the family are making a quick trip to his gran's on Boxing Day. Richard's not coming at all, because — well, he's met this girl who lives close to him and . . ."

"Oh!"

To Tina's amazement, she didn't feel shocked, or even particularly surprised. She looked across at Lee's awkward face full of caring. Concern and a kind of tenderness filled her as she saw how much it had cost him to tell her about Richard's betrayal. The betrayal he didn't even have the courage to admit to her himself.

"How — how long have you had the letter?" she heard herself ask, quietly.

To her surprise, colour flooded Lee's face.

"Er — four days," he admitted, avoiding her eyes again. "I couldn't think of how to tell you, especially with it being Christmas, and besides . . ."

He broke off, and with a little, self conscious shrug added, ". . . I didn't think you'd want to see *me* any more, if — if we couldn't talk about Richard . . ."

"Oh — Lee!" Tina's heart gave a great lurch.

Their eyes met, and then, shyly, they caught each other's fingers across the table. Tina realised the wonderful, amazing truth. For weeks now, these meetings with Lee had been special, just because they were together — learning about each other. Slowly, but surely, beginning to care.

"Richard?" she smiled, happily. "Who's Richard?"

And the happiest Christmas ever had begun.

# Sign

**★ FIRE**

The fire signs are Aries, Leo and Sagittarius and the main characteristics of these peeps are restlessness, forcefulness and ambition. Favourite colours include red, yellow and purple and bold combinations like black and white.

Choose simple uncluttered styles that are easy to move about in — no girlie bows and frills for you lot. This short-legged catsuit teamed with a stretch cotton body is ideal for running around in. Wear it with chunky boots and keep jewellery to a minimum — silver hoop earrings to match the silver hoops on the suit are ideal.

A good night-time choice for girlies on the go is a playsuit. This one looks great with a boxy, cropped jacket. Choose a fabric like velvet — it's v. glam without being too glittery and OTT. Jewellery can be bold and chunky, but make sure it's all the same style.

Choose a hairstyle that's easy to look after — you don't want to have to hang around for ages 'coiffing' your bonce. Keep make-up to a minimum for day, but you can really go to town with bold dark greys and browns for that 'mysterious' party look.

**Stuck in a rut clotheswise, or fed up having one clothes crisis after another? Then let your starsign decide your style. We show you how.**

**★ EARTH**

Taurus, Virgo and Capricorn are the earth signs, and we're sorry to say this, but you're practical, dependable and perhaps just the teensiest bit — em — boring. Earth people (!) favour colours like blue, brown and black and don't like anything too outrageous.

For a daytime style what could be more practical and dependable than good old denim? Save it from being totally ordinary by knotting your shirt over a vest or bra top, and choose a belt with a chunky buckle. Silver hoop earrings and chunky lace-up shoes provide the finishing touches.

For a night painting the town red, out comes faithful old black. You like things that you feel comfortable in, so velvet leggings (a bit posher than cotton ones!) and a bra top are ideal. Cover up with a filmy shirt if you've got any lumps or bumps! We chose an embroidered cotton shirt which'll stay cool when the going gets hot. Let yourself go a little and add some big dangly earrings to finish things off!

Hairstyles like a one length bob are good for practical girlies. You can wear it down, scrunch it up or tie it back without too much fuss and bother. Keep make-up light and natural for day and jazz it up for night with a bolder or bright lipstick and a line of liquid liner along your top eyelid (this takes a *lot* of practice, though, so don't experiment just before you go out!).

**★ WATER**

If your starsign is Cancer, Scorpio or Pisces then you're a water baby, and you're sympathetic, loving and emotional (or should be!). Colours like green, purple, blue, dark red and crimson are what you like to wear.

Choose soft, loose shapes in soft fabrics and muted shades. This moss green swing top in cotton jersey is perfect. Wear it with bleached jeans or opaque cotton tights. Don't overdo things in the jewellery department — just choose one item to focus on, like these earrings here.

For a dressier look we chose a soft floaty blouse in floral chiffon (with *all* your fave colours on it) worn over a black vest top, and a soft stretch velvet mini skirt. A black wool hat and a crochet purse added the finishing touch.

Loose, tumbly wavy hair is best for you. Scrunch it up, roll it loosely or tie back into a pony tail. Try winding some natural rafia around your ponytail and leave lots of ends sticking out (it looks great, honest!). For make-up, muted matt colours are the ones to pick. Greens, browns and heathery purples are all good bets. Keep lip colour matt, too — more stained than actually coloured. For a night time look, just make them slightly stronger than normal.

**★ AIR**

Air signs (Gemini, Libra and Aquarius) are lively and unpredictable. You can't sit still for long and you're not afraid to try new styles and different combinations. You like all sorts of colours, yellow, orange, green and blue being some of the favourites.

For a hardwearing, go anywhere daytime look, jeans are a good bet. Beat boredom by choosing coloured denim like these bright red ones. Team your jeans with chunky boots and then be different by wearing a soft lacy top or crochet jumper with them. For jewellery, choose anything that's eyecatching or unusual.

When you're going out it's no holds barred! Anything that's bright and sparkly is right up your street. A sequinned top like this looks great worn with a black stretchy skirt or velvet hotpants and it's good for dancing around in. Big, flashy earrings complete the look.

When it comes to make-up you like experimenting and you're not afraid of colour. For a daytime look that's not too OTT, try wearing just mascara and a smudge of eyeliner on the eyes with a bright lipstick. For raving, try matching your eyeshadow to what you're wearing, but if it's v. loud and bright be careful how you apply it or you could end up looking like a clown. Hairstyles should be fun and bubbly, and you can use all sorts of things as hair accessories (we used silver pipecleaners here).

Hi!
madonna — vogue

# Bah! HUMBUG!

## A Scrooge Guide to Christmas

**The main thing to remember about a Scrooge-type Christmas is that you *mustn't* enjoy yourself — and you *must* save money! Simple, eh? Well, maybe not. If you're part of a family it could be pretty difficult to copy old Ebenezer — especially if everyone else is determined to have a good time. But it *is* possible if you follow our distinctly *un*festive guide to Christmas!**

Firstly, if you've got a boyfriend, chuck him! That may sound a bit drastic but it's necessary 'cos he'd expect a rather spiffy and expensive (Aaargh!) pressie, wouldn't he? Anyway, you can always make up with him after Christmas — as long as his birthday isn't in January, that is! Once you've done the evil deed, decide how much you *would* have spent on his present and pop the money in your piggy! This is the start of the big saving campaign!

Family and close friends can be more of a problem, but there *are* ways to please everyone.

The best way is to plan *well* ahead and do all your Christmas shopping at the January sales. Things are *much* cheaper then! Another good way to keep your best friend happy without spending a penny, is to go shopping with her and ask her to point out *exactly* what she wants from you. Once she's decided, say that it's just what *you* would like from her and why don't you just buy them now? When she has paid for "yours", "discover" that you don't have enough money with you so suggest your friend keeps the pressie she's bought, and you'll get your own another day. She'll go off happily with her pressie — and it won't have cost you a penny! Cunning, eh?

Cards are even easier than pressies! If you're *really* desperate, you can always dig out the ones you got last year and Tipp-Ex out the names inside — but even for Scroogettes, this is a bit stingy. A better idea is to buy a box of cards *after* Christmas, when they're cheap and, the next year, deliver them all by hand. You'll usually find that after people open their cards they lay them down beside all their others. When their back is turned, you can take the card back and give it to them again next year. If you don't address the envelope and only write "Love from . . ." inside, you can actually give the card to someone *else* the next year. Loads more pennies for the piggy!

If you're a proper Scrooge, you won't feel like decorating the house, but you might have to — to get Mum off your back. But don't despair 'cos decorations don't have to cost the earth! As good old Blue Peter so often tells us, some ultra snazzy deccies can be made from a little tinsel, an old coat hanger and a cut up washing up liquid bottle (empty, of course!). When you've finished you'll be amazed at the result — 'cos it'll look exactly like pieces of washing up liquid bottle fixed to an old wire coat hanger! But at least no one can accuse you of not trying!

Other ways to make Christmas unseasonal include taking the mottos and pressies out of crackers, refusing all party invitations, putting 'No Carol Singers' signs on the window and other killjoy things like that.

On the big day itself, when everyone gets up early to open their presents, you *must* say, "Bah! Humbug! I wanted a long lie!" Then, after dinner (which even Scroogettes won't want to miss), you can settle down to watch the tapes of "The Money Programme" which you've recorded during the year, and then count all the money you've saved by being mean and miserable! What could be better?

**But a word or two of warning. If you follow all this advice you *will* save loads of money, but you'll also lose all your friends, fall out with your family, and have the worst Christmas ever!!!**

D

# JILL'S PHOTO FILE

Dear Jill,
My dad is going on a business trip for three months soon and Mum is going with him. I thought I'd be going, too, but then I discovered that I've to go and stay with Gran.

**JILL SAYS**

You *must* tell your parents exactly how you feel. Sulking, as you've found out, only upsets everyone. Perhaps your parents *should* have discussed things with you, but I'm sure they're doing what they think is best. You may find that Gran is as nervous about having you as you are about staying with her. And how do you know she won't let you go anywhere? If you meet her halfway, you may be pleasantly surprised!

# FORTUNE SPECIAL

## BODY LANGUAGE

Each Starsign rules a part of the body, that part being more vulnerable than normal for those born under the sign associated with it(!).

**ARIES** (Mar. 21-Apr. 19) head.
**TAURUS** (Apr. 20-May 20) throat.
**GEMINI** (May 21-June 20) lungs, neck and shoulders.
**CANCER** (June 21-July 22) chest and stomach.
**LEO** (July 23-Aug. 22) heart.
**VIRGO** (Aug. 23-Sept. 22) abdomen and intestines.
**LIBRA** (Sept. 23-Oct. 22) kidneys and lumbar region.
**SCORPIO** (Oct. 23-Nov. 21) bladder.
**SAGITTARIUS** (Nov. 22-Dec. 21) hips and thighs.
**CAPRICORN** (Dec. 22-Jan. 19) knees.
**AQUARIUS** (Jan. 20-Feb. 18) calves and ankles.
**PISCES** (Feb. 19-Mar. 20) feet.

## Well Handy!

Palmistry is the art of telling what a person's like — and their fortune — by studying their hands and palms. Remember to always use the major hand (i.e. right hand if you're right-handed).

### HANDS

| | |
|---|---|
| Large | intelligence and the ability to carry out skilled work. |
| Small | immaturity, a quick temper and a tendency to gossip. |
| Broad | energy, drive, generosity and a sensible nature. |
| Narrow | shy, sensitive, a bit nervous. |

### FINGERS

| | |
|---|---|
| Flexible (fingers that bend back a lot) | open minded, easy-going. |
| Stiff, unbending | obstinate. |
| Long | indecisive. |
| Short | impuslive. |
| Ring finger (next to little finger) longer than index finger (first finger) | lucky — except where money's concerned. |
| Short index finger | insecurity. |
| Long index finger | luck, money and happiness. |

## Mounts Of The Hand

Look at your hand and you'll see little bumps at the base of the fingers and around the hand. Read on and find out what they mean . . .

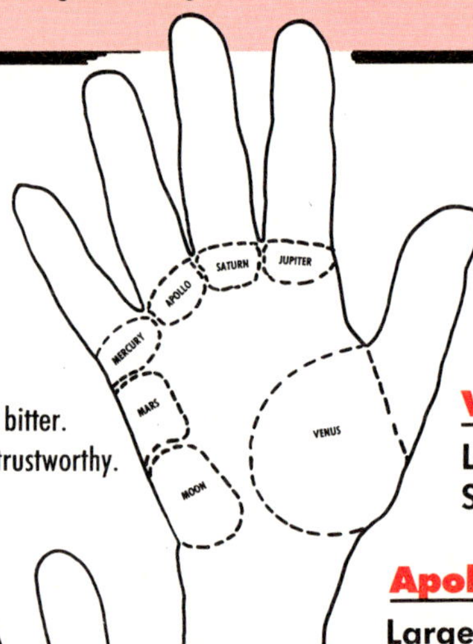


### Jupiter

| | |
|---|---|
| Large | proud and ambitious. |
| Normal | natural, cheerful. |
| Small | underhand, sly. |

### Saturn

| | |
|---|---|
| Large | moody and bitter. |
| Normal | sound and trustworthy. |
| Small | unhappy. |

### Mars

| | |
|---|---|
| Large | determined. |
| Normal | courageous. |
| Small | cowardly. |

### Moon

| | |
|---|---|
| Large | touchy. |
| Normal | romantic. |
| Small | a gossip. |

### Mercury

| | |
|---|---|
| Large | criticises too much. |
| Normal | lively and adventurous. |
| Small | boring. |

### Venus

| | |
|---|---|
| Large mount | affectionate and open. |
| Shallow mount | cold, withdrawn and lacking in energy. |

### Apollo

| | |
|---|---|
| Large | boastful and tendency to exaggerate. |
| Normal | good taste and optimistic. |
| Small | few friends. |

## Lines Of The Palm

Check out the lines on your palm for more info.

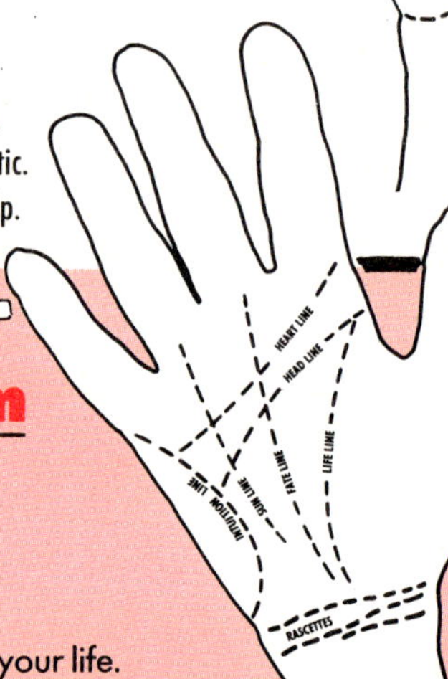


### LIFE LINE

This line relates to energy levels during your life.

| | |
|---|---|
| LONG ,DEEP, NARROW | the best line to have, it promises health, strength and energy. |
| BROKEN LINE | don't worry — this could mean you'll move from a physical job to a desk job — or put lots of energy into a new project. |
| SMALL LINES POINTING UP OFF LIFE LINE | success. |
| LINE FORKS AT THE BOTTOM | you may move to a different country. |

### HEAD LINE

This line indicates vision and judgement.

| | |
|---|---|
| CLEAR STRAIGHT LINE WITH SLIGHT CURVE | determined and strong willed. |
| LINE CURVED UP | money, high standards. |
| FORKED LINE | romantic. |

### LINE OF THE SUN

| | |
|---|---|
| LONG LINE | very lucky — shows an artistic personality and great charm. |

### LINE OF INTUITION

Not many people have this line and it's said to identify people with a spooky sixth sense — i.e. ability to see things that are happening elsewhere(!).

# It's spook city all right . . . cop a loada this lot !

## Leave It Out!

Tea leaf reading's pretty easy. Use a white cup with a wide top and a broad base. Make tea (with leaves — *not* teabags!) in a teapot. Pour a cup of tea and drink it. When there's only about one teaspoonful left, take the cup and swirl it three times, anti-clockwise, towards your heart. Now place the cup upside down on its saucer. Leave it to drain for a while then turn it upright again. Now the fun starts!

Take your time, use your imagination, and try to make something of the leafy, soggy mess you've got. Here's a few suggestions . . .

The handle of the cup stands for home so leaves near here refer to events at home. The rim is for things just about to happen and moving toward the bottom, things are getting more and more into the future.

| | |
|---|---|
| **ACORN** | good health |
| **ANCHOR** | near the top — a nice boyfriend. near the bottom — an unfaithful rat! |
| **APPLE** | good news at school. |
| **BAND** | a party. |
| **BEAR** | danger. |
| **BELL** | good news. |
| **HEART** | look out for the initial of a new hunk. |
| **HEN** | save your cash. |
| **KNIFE** | a fight with friends. |
| **MAN** | a new friend. |
| **PYRAMID** | a secret. |
| **PALM TREE** | a wedding. |
| **ROOF** | away from home for a while. |
| **SCISSORS** | bad moods. |
| **STAR** | happiness and good fortune. |
| **SNAKE** | danger — spiteful friends. |
| **TRIANGLE** | money. |
| **WALKING STICK** | a visitor. |
| **WHEEL** | a gift. |
| **WINDMILL** | a change. |
| **WOLF** | jealous friends. |

## 8 326120 . . . by Numbers!

**Numerologists believe that our fate is determined by certain numbers.**

| 1 | 2 | 3 | 4 | 5 | 6 | 7 | 8 | 9 |
|---|---|---|---|---|---|---|---|---|
| A | B | C | D | E | F | G | H | I |
| J | K | L | M | N | O | P | Q | R |
| S | T | U | V | W | X | Y | Z | |

**Write out your full name with the corresponding chart number next to it like this —**

**J A S O N**
**1+1+1+6+5**
**D O N O V A N**
**4+6+5+6+4+1+5**

**Now add all the numbers together . . . 45.**
**Keep adding until you get a single number . . . 4+5=9.**
**Now read on and see if your personality matches your number.**

**1** An action girl, you're brave, bold and ambitious. You'll take on a top position in any career with all your energy. Never bored, you're a good team leader but some 'ones' could tend to be bossy and try to dominate others.

**2** You're gentle, sensitive, warm . . . not like a one at all. You like to make peace between friends who may argue. You'll like reading, art and music but are easily upset if someone criticises you. It takes a lot to get you angry but when you finally do lose your temper, it's like World War III!

**3** The number of those likely to be actors, dancers, poets or artists is three for sure. You love to be the centre of attention at parties and entertaining. Watch out for jealousy, though.

**4** Sensible and reliable — you'll never let anyone down. Very honest, you'll have great powers of concentration too. You might tend to be a bit too serious and mean with money so be careful!

**5** Fives are charming, restless and always have a whacky plan up their sleeves! They love to travel and have adventures but day-to-day routine bores them silly. Fives might tend to be a bit fickle but they're always good fun.

**6** A six will be honest, cheerful and able to make the best of things. They're also kind and, like twos, peace-loving. They have a great sense of justice and will stick to their guns if they feel a friend has been unfairly treated!

**7** The quiet, nature-loving seven will be a bit of a loner and choose her friends carefully. They make good authors, composers or philosophers although others might find them a bit serious and gloomy.

**8** You're certainly a headstrong one if you're an eight. You've got loads of energy and set high standards for yourself. You'll be quite competitive and used to winning — so used to it that you might get a bit grumpy if you lose!

**9** Nines are quite like eights really — talented, successful and good at making money. They like to see others doing well, so jobs in education, social work and nursing suit them. Nines make good agony aunts — they'll always listen to your problems. They have trouble keeping secrets to themselves, though.

### LINE OF FATE

| | |
|---|---|
| LONG DEEP LINE | fame and fortune. |
| BROKEN LINE | mixed fortunes. |
| CLEAR BREAK IN LINE | change of circumstances. |

### HEART LINE

| | |
|---|---|
| DEEP LINE | warm and loving. |
| CHAINED LINE | changeable feelings. |
| LONG LINE | deep and lasting lurrve. |

### RASCETTES

| | |
|---|---|
| THREE CLEAR LINES | health and wealth. |
| THREE CHAINED LINES | hard work. |

continued from page 19.

# too old! PART TWO

When the film ended —
THAT WAS TERRIFIC, WASN'T IT, LYNN?
MMM. YEAH!
EXCEPT I DIDN'T UNDERSTAND ANY OF IT. I GAVE UP TRYING TO READ THE SUBTITLES AND WATCH THE FILM AT THE SAME TIME AFTER THE FIRST FIVE MINUTES.
HOW ABOUT A COFFEE BEFORE I SEE YOU HOME, LYNN?
CIRCLE
I'D LOVE THAT, B-BUT —
HE'S GONNA THINK I'M A REAL BABY.
MY FOLKS ARE A BIT FUNNY, YOU SEE. THEY'LL GO BANANAS IF I DON'T GET HOME SOON.
THAT'S NO PROBLEM, LYNN. LOTS OF PARENTS ARE LIKE THAT. I'LL DELIVER YOU STRAIGHT TO YOUR DOOR.
And —
OH, LYNN, IT'S GREAT BEING WITH YOU. YOU WILL COME OUT WITH ME AGAIN, WON'T YOU?
'COURSE I WILL, TOM.
TRY STOPPING ME!
MY MATE'S HAVING A PARTY NEXT SATURDAY. IT SHOULD BE GREAT AND I WON'T MIND IF WE HAVE TO LEAVE A BIT EARLIER THAN THE OTHERS . . .
Then —
IS THIS REALLY HAPPENING TO ME?

**continued on page 82.**

# LOOKIN' GOOD...

## We asked some of our fave models for their style and beauty tips . . .

### KEZIA

**STYLE**

I like classic styles — usually I stick to dark colours with some red and white things. I don't have a lot of clothes but when I do buy something I'll spend a bit more and make sure it goes with a few other things I've got.

**BEAUTY**

I walk instead of taking the bus, when I can — and I try to drink lots of water. I'm quite lucky — I don't have any fillings at all so I'm trying to keep things that way. I carry a toothbrush and toothpaste with me so I can brush my teeth when I've been eating sweets. I don't really watch my diet, but I'm a black belt in karate so that keeps me in shape (I hope!). I dab any spots with astringent then try to leave them alone. I stand on my head for a minute before bedtime — I read somewhere that it helps the skin on your face because all the blood goes to your head. I don't know if it works but I've been trying it anyway! I never wear make-up unless it's for a photo session and I have my hair cut regularly.

### REBECCA

**STYLE**

I usually have my hair down and I'm never out of my jeans.

**BEAUTY**

Since I started modelling I've become a lot more interested in beauty. One thing I always do is remove any make-up before bed. I cleanse, tone and moisturise my skin every day. I also condition my hair after every wash.

### SUSIE

**STYLE**

I'm always borrowing things from my boyfriend. He's into trendy casual stuff — jeans and sweatshirts mostly. I buy loads of shoes which sets me back a bit but I don't spend a lot on make-up. Our school has an annual ball that's always good fun 'cos you get really dressed up.

**BEAUTY**

My hair's permed so I have to look after the condition. I work in a baker's shop on Saturdays which is really bad news for my diet — well, I don't really diet anyway. I try to use body lotion after baths to stop my skin drying out. As for spots, I just try to live with them and hope Karen, the "Hi!" make-up artist, can cover them up!

### STEPHANIE

**STYLE**

I mostly wear black which is pretty boring, really. I just can't seem to snap out of it! I like most of the clothes I model for "Hi!".

**BEAUTY**

I always use cosmetics and toiletries that are cruelty-free. I think that's really important. I don't eat sweets if I can help it, but I can't stand diet drinks so I just go for the 'fat' ones and try not to feel guilty! I'm determined to keep going to aerobics this year.

### ALISON

**STYLE**

My wardrobe is totally disorganised — nothing seems to go with anything else! I've got loads of accessories all over my room too. It's because I'm always buying things on impulse — then regretting it later. My trainers are my favourites. I always wear them.

**BEAUTY**

I don't wear make-up during the week so my face gets a rest! I like trying new beauty products and treatments so I'm always in Boots checking out the new ranges. I've got a bike so I go for runs on that in the summer.

# THE VALLEY GIRLS

YOU ever fallen madly in love at first sight? I did the other week — with the most fab, wicked dress in the entire cosmiverse! There it was in Denham's window, black and gold, body-hugging. As soon as I saw it, I *wanted* it!

Trust my mates Linda, Zoe and Bev to bring me back down to earth, though.

"Come on, Kay, how're you going to afford it? It's almost twenty-five quid!" they pointed out. "And you're skint."

I didn't need telling that last bit. I'm *always* skint. Even with my Saturday job I never have enough cash. Still — like I said, I was in love. I had to have that dress!

"It *is* dead glam," Bev sighed. "Hope the stuff in our fashion show'll be like that."

This fashion show was something our school was putting on. They were getting all the local boutiques and big stores to lend them clothes, and all the proceeds from the show were going to the local hospital to help build a new wing. We were all looking forward to it, and Bev had been dieting like mad for days in the hope that she'd get picked to be one of the models. Lin and Zoe were keen to try out for models too. I'd been interested — but right now, all I could think of was earning the dosh to buy my dress.

"Odd jobs," suggested Lin. She's my best mate. "Walk dogs, babysit, that sort of stuff."

I pulled a face. I get enough of babysitting at home, what with our Mark and Paula and baby Kylie. Still, I wanted that dress!

Between us we worked out some charges. Fifty pence for dog walking, £1 for washing a car, 30p for going shopping, and I started knocking on doors in the Valley. And I got work. Lin helped. We weeded gardens, washed cars, did all sorts. I also got an ear bashing from nosy old Granny Porter, that I used to live next door to, about how when *she* was a girl *she* worked hard and didn't expect any paying for it! She can talk. They didn't *have* cars to wash and polish in those days. They'd only just invented the wheel!

FOR a whole week, I really did work hard. And at the end of it, I had over twelve quid to show for my efforts. I even did some babysitting — for Zoe's twin niece and nephew, Lisa and James. Vanessa, their mum, wanted Zoe to do it, but it was Youth Club night and Zoe wasn't keen. So I gave up the chance of the Youth Club to spend an evening with *two* babies even younger than Kylie.

"You're a pal, Kay," Zoe enthused.

"I'm a berk," I muttered.

A whole evening! And would Lisa go to sleep? As I rocked her, cooed at her, waved her teddy bear at her for what seemed like hours, I kept thinking of my dress. With the two quid Vanessa had promised me I was well over halfway to owning it!

On the following morning I went to Denham's to check it was still there, like I did every day. And it had gone! I rushed into the store to check — perhaps they'd just taken it out of display. But no — they'd sold it. And it was the last one. The *very* last.

I could have howled. Why hadn't I asked them to hold it for me? But I knew they wouldn't have — not when I couldn't guarantee how long it'd take me to get the money.

"Never mind, Kay," Bev consoled me. "The fashion show's coming up

# A SPECIAL PROSE STORY

soon and maybe you'll see something in it you'll like."

I wasn't so hopeful. Nothing could match up to my black and gold dress. I lost interest in the show at that point, and when it came to the auditions for models, I probably wouldn't have gone if Lin hadn't dragged me along with her for support.

BEV was really nervous. She'd stayed off fried foods, chocolate, chips, crisps and doughnuts for nearly two weeks, and she'd lost six pounds. We were all proud of her and hoped it'd be enough for her to be picked.

It wasn't. Mrs Sanders, the Domestic Science Teacher, was doing the auditioning, and she picked only the skinniest girls — like Zoe. Even Lin didn't make it, so poor Bev wasn't alone — but she *was* disappointed. She disappeared off to the tuckshop afterwards and came out with two packets of crisps to cheer herself up. Lin cheered *herself* up by putting her name down to be a dresser on the night.

"At least we're helping to dress the models, and we'll be handling all the fab gear," she confided.

"We?" I queried.

Linda grinned and linked her arm in mine.

"It'll help you get over your tragic loss," she said.

"Oh, ha ha," I grimaced.

By the day of the fashion show, though, I was looking forward to being a dresser. The clothes arrived from the various stores during the morning and Mrs Sanders had them all taken straight to the textiles room. At lunchtime, we couldn't resist it!

"Just a quick peek," Zoe whispered as we watched Mrs Sanders leave the room and head for the canteen and her lunch.

We crept in. There were outfits draped everywhere, hanging from doors, laid out on benches. Dresses, skirts, tops, trousers, scarves, jackets, leggings — you name it.

"Kay — *look*!" cried Lin. "It's your dress!"

Well, it wasn't exactly. It was the same sort of style, but a sort of rich burgundy-wine colour. Still, it wasn't bad. I took it carefully off its hanger and held it against myself.

"It's beautiful!" breathed Bev.

It was, too. It was from In-Wear, and its price label said £29.99.

Thirty quid. More than my original dress. And I still only had fourteen. Oh, well — I can dream, can't I?

"Look out!" gasped Zoe from the door. "Prefects! They're coming to check up on the stuff!"

We put the clothes down and scarpered, smartish. We didn't want to get banned from the show. Bev was starting to feel really sorry that she hadn't put her name down to be a dresser, too.

"I'm going to be the only one of us not doing anything tonight," she mourned as we walked back to school that evening, for the show.

"*Wow*!" Zoe gasped suddenly. "Who's *he*?"

Some guy was outside the school gates unloading sound equipment from a van. He was quite nice looking — sort of like Jordan, from New Kids.

"I heard the DJ from the local hospital radio's going to do the commentating for our show. Bet that's him," said Lin.

We had to drag Zoe away. She was practically drooling. We hurried her into the room backstage in the Hall which was going to be the changing area, where all the models and dressers were already preparing. Mrs Sanders and other women were fussing around — I guessed they were from the shops, there to keep an eye on the clothes. We didn't notice in all the bustle that Bev had disappeared . . .

WE got Zoe into her first outfit, the show started and off she pranced. I was pretty impressed — she really could walk like a model. We could hear the music and the DJ's voice. "Zoe is wearing a lycra skirt and leggings and . . ."

His voice was as dishy as he was.

A minute later Zoe was back, flushed and excited.

"Guess where Bev is?" she panted as she stripped off at lightning speed. "She's *only* got herself a job with Jordan, hasn't she!"

For a moment I didn't twig. Then I got it. Bev was helping out the DJ! Handing him his notes and stuff! She'd obviously seen her chance, and gone for it!

"Wish it was *me*!" Zoe sighed as Linda tried to zip her into her next outfit — the burgundy dress. "Lucky old Bev — *ow*!"

"Oh, crikey!" Lin gasped suddenly. The zip had torn, just come apart in her hand. Lin stood there in speechless horror as Mrs Sanders and another woman swept down on her.

I thought she was going to get blown up. But all they did was grab safety pins and cobble the zip back together, swifter than you could see, and shove Zoe out to the catwalk.

"S-sorry," Lin mumbled, brick red.

"These things happen," said the woman. "Must have been a faulty zip. That dress will have to go in our next half price sale."

My mind raced. I've never done a division sum so quickly in my entire life! I almost grabbed her arm.

"Please!" I panted. If you're selling it for fifteen, could I buy it? I've got fourteen already, and I'll mend the zip and . . ."

The woman smiled.

"Well, if you're prepared to mend the zip yourself, I should think you could have it for fourteen," she said.

They must have heard my shriek of delight out on the catwalk!

What a brilliant evening that turned out! Zoe was flying high from all the applause she'd been getting. Lin was pretty pleased with herself, too.

"Bags I borrow that dress, seeing as it was me who bust the zip for you — even if I didn't mean to!" she laughed.

I laughed too, hugging my dress. I've never owned anything half so fabulous!

And Bev? She was in *heaven*! "Jordan" had not only let her hand him his notes, he'd let her put a couple of records on, and at the end he'd thanked her publicly. *And* he'd kissed her on the cheek! I don't think our Bev'll come back to earth for days!

Hope we have a fashion show again soon!

# A QUESTION OF SPORT

**Is your most strenuous activity reaching for the remote control to change the telly channels? It is? Shame on you! Okay — now's the time to stop being a couch potato and start being a jumping bean! We've got the gen if you've got the energy!**

## GET IN THE SWIM

Swimming is soooo good for you — it's probably the best all-round exercise there is. It uses almost all the muscles in the body, but because your body is supported by the water, there's very little chance of overdoing things or pulling a muscle. One thing not to do, though, is go for a swim after a heavy meal. Always allow at least two hours after eating, otherwise you'll probably be doubled up with painful stomach cramps just when you want to impress that particularly hunky pool attendant!

Most schools have a swimming pool or access to one, so this is probably the easiest way to take part, just for fun or on a competitive level. But maybe you want to take things further? If you want to compete, other than at school, you should join a swimming club which is a member of the Amateur Swimming Association. Write to them — Amateur Swimming Association, Harold Fern House, Derby Square, Loughborough, Leicestershire, LE11 0AL — for information on the club nearest to you. Who knows — you could be the next Zara Lang!

## TIE YOURSELF IN KNOTS

Believe it or not, that's one thing you *won't* do if you take up yoga. What you *will* do though is tone up your body and become more supple. Lots of yoga pictures you see in magazines and books look very difficult, but that's probably because they're advanced exercises. There are loads of easy yoga postures which are taught to beginners. The easiest one of all is simply lying flat on your back with your eyes closed! Besides toning up the body and internal organs (oo-er!), yoga is great for relaxing the mind. It's just the thing to do after you've been wrestling with your Maths homework or having a mega row with your boyfriend!

The great thing is you can do it at home using a book as a guide. It's probably best, though, to join a class. That way, your teacher can make sure that you're doing everything properly — otherwise you *might* end up tying yourself in knots! Phone your local authority for a list of yoga classes in your area or write to the British Wheel of Yoga, 1 Hamilton Place, Boston Road, Sleaford, Lincolnshire, NG34 7ES for more information.

## ON YER BIKE

Like swimming, cycling is a good all-round exercise — and there's very little chance of causing strains and sprains. It's also a great (and cheap!) way of getting around. So instead of propping up your nearest bus stop every morning, you could whizz past on your bike, fetchingly attired in snazzy cycling shorts, of course!

If you're a teensy bit overweight (What? Never!), then cycling is a really effective form of exercise. The body weight is distributed, so it's much better for you than running,

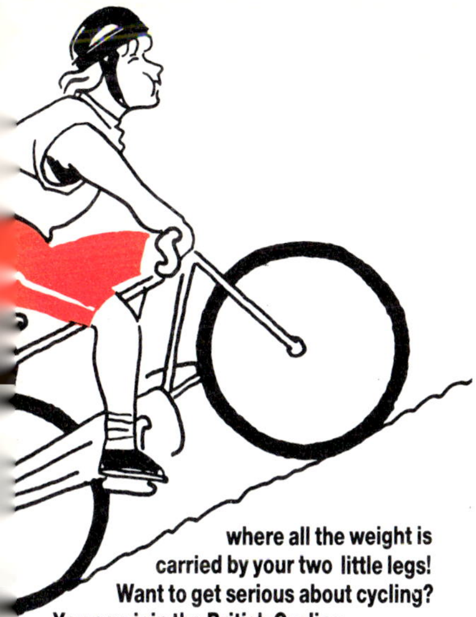

where all the weight is carried by your two little legs! Want to get serious about cycling? You can join the British Cycling Federation as a juvenile member (under 16) by writing to the British Cycling Federation, 36 Rockingham Road, Kettering, Northants NN16 8NG.

## CHOP! CHOP!

There's more to karate than chopping bricks in half with your bare hands, y'know! And you don't have to speak with a Japanese accent either! Karate is a Japanese martial art. Martial means warlike (oo-er!), but karate is usually simply practised as a sport or for self-defence.

Modern karate is a striking system, using high energy kicks, punches and strikes as weapons. Sounds painful, doesn't it?! But karate is very controlled, so no one should actually be hurt when the sport is properly supervised. Depending on how good you are, karate is graded into different coloured belts, ranging from a yellow belt to a black belt. One of the "Hi!" models is a black belt, so no one messes with her!

Your local council will have details on classes in your area and for more information you could visit your library or write to The Martial Arts Commission, 1st Floor, Broadway House, 15-16 Deptford, Broadway, London SE8 4PE.

## GEE UP

The most important thing about taking up horse-riding is that you've got to like horses! The other thing is that it can cost quite a lot of money. Lessons vary quite a bit in price but you should expect to pay about £10 an hour for coaching and around £8 an hour for an accompanied ride. You don't have to buy any special gear to start with. A reputable riding stable will provide you with a hard hat, which is essential. You should make sure you wear sturdy boots or shoes and comfortable jeans.

Most riding schools encourage you to help out — which usually means mucking out the stables (!) — but this isn't compulsory. Write to The British Horse Society, British Equestrian Centre, Stoneleigh, Kenilworth, Warwickshire CV8 2LR for lots of information and details of how to join the Pony Club.

## GYM'LL FIX IT

Ever since Olga Korbut (mega famous Russian gymnast) appeared on our TV screens way back in 1972, gymnastics in Britain has been growing in leaps and bounds (har! har!). There are over four and a half million people, most of them girls, performing gymnastics in Britain today. If a new gymnastics club opened every day of the year for the next year, there would still be a waiting list. Phew!

The best way to get into gymnastics is through your school — and the younger you are the better. The benefits of doing gymnastics are pretty obvious — apart from being able to impress all your mates by doing the splits! It builds stamina and strength and makes your body supple and graceful. If you'd like more information, speak to your P.E. teacher or write to the British Schools' Gymnastics Association, 26 Broom Acres, Sandhurst, Camberley, Surrey GU17 8PW.

## GO FOR IT

If you're really adventurously minded, you could have a go at lots of different and unusual sports — like wind-surfing and abseiling! PGL Adventure Holidays for children and teenagers are jam-packed with exciting activities, including canoeing, skiing, archery, go-karting, mountain biking, wind-surfing and abseiling!

All the sports are tried and tested and safety is of prime importance, whether you're scaling a cliff face or riding the rapids. PGL welcome anyone from age three to eighteen and you can choose the adventure holiday which most appeals to you.

For a free brochure, write to PGL Young Adventure Ltd., Alton Court, Penyard Lane, Ross-on-Wye, Herefordshire HR9 5NR.

## BOOGIE ON

Okay, you lazy lot — if you can't work up any enthusiasm for any of the sports and activities mentioned, all is not lost! Get down to your local disco and boogie! Dancing is one of the best forms of exercise and burns up loads of calories. It's fabby fun as well, of course!

# Ashamed To Say...

Rachel could just picture the scene.
A VET — OR A JOURNALIST? THE WAY RACHEL'S BEEN ACTING LATELY, SHE'LL BE LUCKY TO PASS A SINGLE EXAM!
IT'S GOING TO BE AWFUL! POOR MUM'LL DIE OF EMBARRASSMENT!
I'M VERY PLEASED TO MEET YOU, MRS MILLER. CAROLINE'S ONE OF MY STAR PUPILS.
WE'RE SO PROUD OF HER, MR ROSS.
SWOT!
I WISH THERE WAS SOME WAY TO STOP MUM FINDING OUT HOW USELESS I AM. SHE'S GONE THROUGH ENOUGH LATELY.
The night before the parents' evening —
WHAT DO YOU THINK I SHOULD WEAR TOMORROW NIGHT, LOVE?
I-I DUNNO, MUM. LOOK, THERE'S NOT THAT MANY PARENTS ACTUALLY GOING. LISA'S MUM AND DAD CAN'T MAKE IT, AND . . .
YOU'RE ASHAMED OF ME, AREN'T YOU?
W-WHAT?

THAT'S WHY YOU DON'T WANT ME AT THE PARENTS' EVENING! IS IT BECAUSE I'M ON MY OWN NOW? OR THE WAY I LOOK? OR DRESS?
OH — MUM!
IT'S NOT YOU I'M ASHAMED OF! IT'S ME! I JUST CAN'T DO THE THINGS YOU WANT ME TO. I-I'M NOT CLEVER ENOUGH! I DO TRY, BUT IT'S JUST NOT ENOUGH.
I STARTED TO FALL BEHIND WHEN DAD WAS ILL, AND SOMEHOW, I'VE JUST NEVER CAUGHT UP. I'VE GOT TO WORK REALLY HARD — JUST TO SCRAPE BY!
OH, RACHEL, WHY DIDN'T YOU TELL ME? WE COULD HAVE SORTED THIS ALL OUT AGES AGO!
I'LL BE PROUD OF YOU, NO MATTER HOW YOU DO AT SCHOOL OR WHAT YOU DECIDE TO BE. OKAY?
OKAY, MUM . . . AND THANKS
NOW, ARE YOU GOIND TO HELP ME DECIDE WHAT TO WEAR, OR NOT?
SURE!
I'M ALMOST LOOKING FORWARD TO PARENTS' EVENING, NOW! AND WITH MUM'S BACKING I'M SURE MY WORK WILL IMPROVE NOW!

# MIGHTY BITES!

We asked some stars (and Liz!) what their most favourite super soaraway sandwiches were and put them to the test. Here's the results.

| NAMES | FILLING | ORIGINALITY | TASTE | EAT ABILITY | SCOFF STARS |
|---|---|---|---|---|---|
| TREVOR | Stilton, mango and walnut. | Mmm — very posh. Not at all Trevor and Simonish. | Don't know about the stinky Stilton, but the mango and walnut is lovely. | Very wiffy. Clothes pegs on noses if you don't like Stilton. Bit squidgy. | * If you hate Stilton. **** If you like it. |
| SIMON | Prawn and avocado. | Fairly common, but classy. | Very nice — if you like avocado. | Really mushy and oozed out of the sides. | *** |
| JASON D | Vegemite, peanut butter, pickle, ham, cheese, lettuce and alfalfa sprouts. | V. original, but sounds completely disgusting. | Didn't even want to taste this! | Stuffed full with all sorts of stuff falling out. Really messy. | * |
| CHRIS LOWE (PET SHOP BOYS) | Chips and tomato sauce on white bread with marg. | Not original at all. | Mmm — lovely! There's nothing better than a fat chip butty! | Dead easy. The chips squashed down a treat. Only slight sauce fall out. | ***** |
| MARTIKA | Chicken and avocado. | Has she been copying Simon? | Not quite as nice as the prawn one. | Mushy avocado again! | ** |
| LIZ | Chicken and grape with tarragon mayo. | Almost as snootsome as Trevor. | Most delicious! | Not too bad. Lost some lettuce and one grape! | **** |

**OVERALL RATINGS**

As you can see from our chart, Jase eats the most blee-gusting sarnies *ever* — give us a chip butty any day!

I DON'T KNOW WHY YOU'RE PUTTING UP THAT STUPID ADVENT CALENDAR, MO. IT'S A WASTE OF TIME.
NO, IT ISN'T. I LIKE COUNTING DOWN TO CHRISTMAS DAY.

# COUNTDOWN

IT'S CHRISTMAS EVE AND THE CHRISTMAS DISCO I'M LOOKING FORWARD TO. EVERYBODY'S GOING.
NOT EVERYBODY, HELEN. I'M NOT.
BUT YOU CAN'T MISS THIS. IT'S THE BEST DISCO OF THE YEAR — AND ALL YOUR FRIENDS ARE GOING.
YEAH, BUT THEY'RE ALL GOING WITH THEIR BOYFRIENDS.
AH, SOMETHING YOU'RE SHORT OF AT THE MOMENT.
RIGHT! IF I WENT TO THAT DISCO, I'D BE ON MY OWN ALL NIGHT. EVERYONE ELSE IS PAIRED UP.
DON'T GIVE UP YET. YOU'VE STILL GOT TWENTY FOUR DAYS TO FIND A DATE.
OH GREAT, HELEN — BUT HOW?

The next morning, December the first —
OH LOOK, THE FIRST DOOR IN MY CALENDAR'S A SNOWMAN.
WOW, AND I WAS EXPECTING A PALM TREE!
DON'T BE SO SARKY. ACTUALLY, THIS HAS GIVEN ME AN IDEA FOR MEETING A BOY.
WHAT'RE YOU GOING TO DO? FLY TO THE NORTH POLE AND GET A DATE WITH AN ESKIMO?
BETTER THAN THAT. THE NEW ICE CREAM PARLOUR IN THE PRECINCT MUST BE A GOOD BET FOR FINDING A GUY. I'LL EVEN LET YOU COME ALONG FOR SUPPORT.
SUPER! I GET VOLUNTEERED FOR ALL THE BEST JOBS.
Later —
BUT I DON'T REALLY FANCY ICE CREAM. IT'S DECEMBER, AFTER ALL.
OH STOP MOANING, HELEN! IT'S IN A GOOD CAUSE.
I SHOULD'VE THOUGHT OF THIS BEFORE. THE PLACE WILL BE FULL OF GOOD LOOKING GUYS ANY MINUTE.
WELL, I HOPE THEY HURRY UP! I DON'T THINK I CAN EAT MUCH MORE OF THIS STUFF.
But two hours and three sundaes later —
HMM! I DON'T THINK THIS IS WORKING. THE PLACE IS FULL OF KIDS, THERE ISN'T A HUNK IN SIGHT AND HELEN HAS TURNED A FUNNY SHADE OF GREEN.

A few days later —
HEY, A STAR. THAT GIVES ME AN IDEA.
OH YEAH? NOW YOU WANT TO GO OUT WITH CAPTAIN KIRK, I SUPPOSE.
NO, STUPID. I THOUGHT WE COULD TRY THE STARLIGHT CLUB IN THE TOWN CENTRE.
THERE'S ONE TEENY PROBLEM — YOU HAVE TO BE OVER SIXTEEN TO GET IN.
PHOOEY! A MINOR DETAIL! WITH DECENT MAKE-UP AND THE RIGHT CLOTHES, I COULD PASS FOR SIXTEEN NO PROBS!
She didn't!
WHO'RE YOU TRYING TO KID? CLEAR OFF HOME AND PLAY WITH YOUR BARBIE DOLL.
WHY DID I LET MYSELF GET TALKED INTO THIS? IT'S S-O-O-O-O EMBARRASSING!
As the days passed —
HELEN'S BEEN KEEPING OUT OF MY WAY, BUT I DON'T NEED HER HELP. I'M SURE I CAN CRACK THIS ON MY OWN.
HMM, CAROL SINGERS! WELL, THE YOUTH CLUB USUALLY ORGANISES A CAROL CONCERT. I'M NOT ALL THAT INTERESTED BUT . . .

. . . GORGEOUS ROBIN ARMSTRONG IS IN THE CHOIR. IF I COULD JUST GET CLOSE TO HIM, WE COULD MAKE REALLY BEAUTIFUL MUSIC TOGETHER . . . ALL I HAVE TO DO IS SPEAK TO MISS WILSON, THE CLUB LEADER.
So —
MISS WILSON, I'VE BEEN THINKING. I'D LIKE TO JOIN THE CHOIR.
OH YES? AND WHAT'S BROUGHT THIS ON?
THE FESTIVE SEASON, I THINK. I ENJOY SINGING CHRISTMAS CAROLS.
WELL IT'S A BIT LATE, MO. THE CHOIR'S BEEN REHEARSING FOR WEEKS.
BUT COULDN'T YOU SQUEEZE IN JUST ONE MORE?
I SUPPOSE A RESERVE MIGHT BE A GOOD IDEA, JUST IN CASE ANY OF THE CHOIR GO DOWN WITH SOMETHING. COME IN HERE. I'LL GIVE YOU AN AUDITION.
GREAT! ALL I NEED NOW IS A FLU EPIDEMIC.
But —
GOOD GRIEF, MO! I ASKED YOU TO SING A SCALE, NOT A RANDOM COLLECTION OF FLAT NOTES.

I SUPPOSE IT'S BACK TO THE DRAWING BOARD, OR IN MY CASE THE ADVENT CALENDAR.
A few days later —
YOU'RE NOT STILL AT THAT, ARE YOU? DON'T YOU EVER GIVE UP?
NO. I'M SURE THIS'LL BE A BIG HELP. IN FACT, THIS COULD BE IT!
SEE — CHRISTMAS DECORATIONS!
HOW'S THAT GONNA HELP?
ON SATURDAYS ROBIN ARMSTRONG HELPS OUT ON HIS UNCLE'S STALL IN THE MARKET, AND AT THIS TIME OF YEAR, THEY ALWAYS SELL CHRISTMAS DECCIES.
Helen was 'persuaded' to go with Jo —
ALL I'VE GOT TO DO IS MAKE ROBIN NOTICE ME THEN I'LL ASK HIM TO THE DISCO.
WELL, DON'T SING TO HIM, WHATEVER YOU DO!
THERE'S ONLY ONE THING WRONG WITH YOUR PLAN — ROBIN ISN'T HERE.
BUT HE MUST BE! HE ALWAYS HELPS OUT. PERHAPS HE'S JUST GONE ON AN ERRAND.

EXCUSE ME, WILL ROBIN BE BACK SOON?
NO. HE'S AT SOME FLAMIN' OLD PEOPLE'S HOME WITH SOME STUPID CHOIR GIVING A CAROL CONCERT TO A BUNCH OF DEAF OLD FOGGIES!
I'D FORGOTTEN ABOUT THE CAROL CONCERT.
YOU SHOULD'VE GONE TO WOOLWORTH'S FOR DECORATIONS LIKE EVERYONE ELSE.
On Christmas Eve —
A NATIVITY SCENE! THAT'S NO HELP AT ALL — UNLESS THREE WISE MEN ARE ABOUT TO KNOCK ON THE DOOR AND GIVE ME A CUNNING PLAN ON HOW TO GET ROBIN TO NOTICE ME.
MORE CHRISTMAS CARDS! OH, THERE'S ONE FOR ME.
THERE'S A TICKET INSIDE FOR THE DISCO! "SEE YOU THERE — LOVE, ROBIN. "OH, WOW! THAT'S GREAT!
A few blocks away, a certain Robin Armstrong had received a very similar onvelope —
"SEE YOU THERE, LOVE, MO." I NEVER REALISED SHE WAS INTERESTED. HEY, THIS IS FANTASTIC!
GAP
ALL RIGHT, I ADMIT IT. I SENT **BOTH** THOSE CARDS. BUT IT IS THE SEASON OF GOODWILL, ISN'T IT? AND THAT INCLUDES LITTLE SISTERS LIKE MO!
THE END

# BEAUTY

## and the balaclava (!?)

**When it's cold and miserable there's loads you can do in the beauty department to keep you looking hot (aside from stuffing your bonce into a balaclava — not advised for trendy chicks)!**

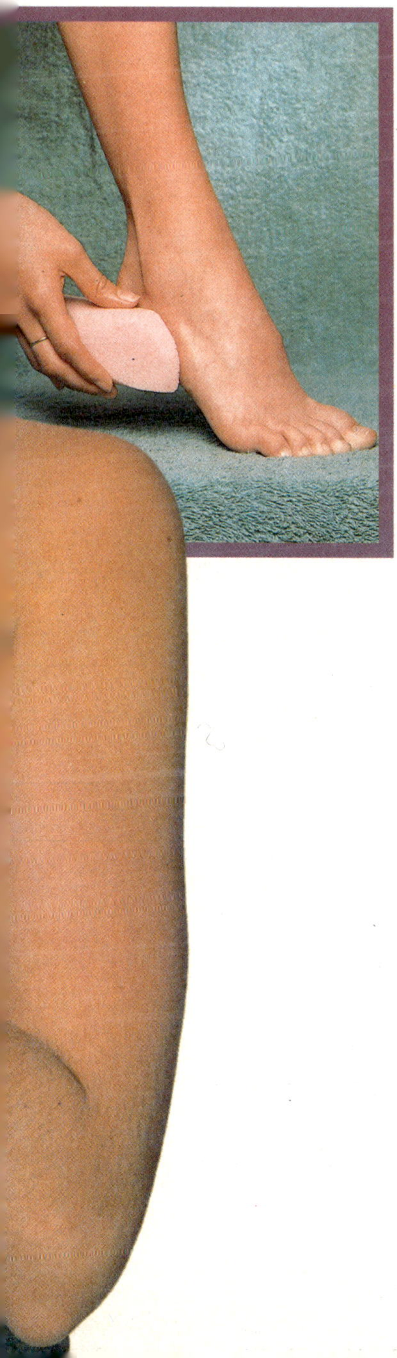

### FACE

Winter brings wind, cold and all sorts of nasties for your face to deal with! Even inside, central heating can really make your skin dry out. Now's definitely the time to stick to a skin care routine for your face (no sneaking off to bed after the Christmas parties with your make-up still on). Cleanse, tone and moisturise or, if you prefer, use a mild soap and water, then moisturise. Do this twice a day and you should stay in the clear. Invest in some Vaseline or zinc and castor oil cream (available from Boots) as these are both good all-round protectors for lips and anywhere skin can be dry and flaky (eg. the nose area!). After moisturising at night, smooth some over the affected area and you'll find it prevents the moisture from escaping, leaving you with lovely soft skin in the morning. These are also a good treat for eyelashes (apply gently), keeping them well conditioned. Winter make-up should be quite subtle — try using matt shades rather than sparkly colours for a natural effect.

### HANDS

Hands and nails need to be looked after in cold weather too. Look out for a rich hand and nail moisturiser to give them a treat. Try not to put v. cold hands in front of a hot fire. It's much better to let them warm up slowly. Nails can be strengthened with clear nail polish. You'll probably go through around 10 pairs of gloves this winter by the time you've left some on the bus etc. (don't we all) but don't go out in the cold without 'em!

### BODY

Just because your body's mostly covered up in winter doesn't mean you can forget about it! You still want to be smooth, blemish free and lovely next summer, don't you? Yup — then remember to use an exfoliating body scrub once in a while to keep the skin fresh, and look for a moisturising bath foam or add some baby oil to your bath. (You can use baby oil after a shower, while you're still wet, to stop the skin becoming dry.) Using a body lotion isn't a bad idea — you can buy some nice ones that smell great from the Body Shop. Make sure you're getting regular exercise to keep you fit and try not to resort to stodgy food and chocs just because it's cold!

### HAIR

You'll probably find that your hair won't grow as quickly in the winter but still try to have it trimmed every six weeks or so to keep it in shape. Using conditioner every time you wash should help you stop getting the 'frizzies' in wet weather. Trying to cut down on products? There are lots of all-in-one formulas available now which can be used both as styling aids (while the hair is wet) and fixing sprays to hold. Chances are the wind will play havoc with anything that's fixed into place so try to pick a style which allows some movement. After conditioning, try rinsing with cold water (if you can stand it!). This acts as a toner, flattening the hair cuticle (outer layer) for more shine.

### FEET

Being tucked away inside socks and shoes or boots all the time doesn't give your feet much chance to breathe so try to pad about with bare feet at night for a while if you can. Any rough skin should be rubbed away with a pumice stone or a nice rough soap bar (like Cosmetics To Go's Sandbar, phone 0800 373 366 for details). Corns — lumps of tough skin on toes — and Athlete's foot — an infection causing very itchy feet — should both be treated early to avoid *major* discomfort! You'll find a great range of foot care products at Boots.

Always make sure that your feet are completely dry after a bath (use talc between the toes) and try a soothing foot lotion with peppermint or menthol as a treat. Never wear the same socks or tights twice!

***Last of all, remember to keep nice 'n' cosy this winter — and no, wearing a warm jumper won't make you look fat! Anyway, better that than snuffling around with a cold at Crimbo!***

# I WANN

**Okay, so you want to be a pop star, but everyone knows it's a long, hard slog to the top and not everyone makes it, right? Wrong! Play our nifty game and you could become a mega star in approximately one hour! Yes, it's true! On the other hand, you could end up 'Down the Dumper', ha, ha! What a shame!**

**Just throw a dice to move round the board and when you land on a pop star or cosmic pattern square, follow the appropriate direction. Easy!**

## DIRECTIONS

**3.** You've sent off loads of demo tapes to record companies and, hooray, Rip-off Records want to hear more. Have another turn.

**4.** You get chatting to a girl on the bus who says she's Whitney Houston's cousin. She also says she can fix it for you to meet Whitney. Move forward 4.

**7.** Your tape recorder chews up your new demo for Rip-off. Go back 1 space.

**10.** You win a fab and groovy keyboard in a competition. Now you too can play like Adamski! Move forward 2.

**11.** You find a tenner in the pocket of a jacket you haven't worn for ages. Now you can afford to have your tape recorder fixed. Move on 1.

**13.** New Kids need some girlie backing singers for their latest tour and you get an audition. Unfortunately, you fail miserably. Go back 5 spaces.

**16.** In a fit of generosity, Dad buys you some blank tapes so that you can make another demo. Move forward 2 spaces.

**20.** You get tangled up in your baggy breeks whilst perfecting your MC Hammer hip-hop style. Miss a turn.

**21.** It's a lovely sunny day. Go out and post your new demo. (But stay where you are on the board!)

**22.** You go to visit an image consultancy and they come up with a fabby new look for you. Move on 4.

**26.** You wake up to find your funky false eye lashes stuck to the pillow. The new look is right out the window! Go back 1 space.

**30.** Prince has heard your demo, thinks you're fabulous and asks you to marry him. Yo! You have *arrived*! Leap forward 6 spaces!

**33.** Rip-off Records offer you a recording contract. Yes — it's all happening now! Have another turn.

**35.** The Pet Shop Boys want to produce your first single — but so does Prince. There's a big fight. Go back 3.

**37.** Your first single is released — a double A side produced by Prince *and* the Petties. Move on 3.

**38.** Oops — you've been associated with Yell! (remember them?) therefore losing all pop credibility. Go back to the start.

**41.** George Michael phones up and asks you out to dinner at a Swanko de Posh restaurant. You accept. Move forward 2 spaces.

**45.** Prince hears about your date with George and gives you the flick. Boo, hoo! Go back 5.

**47.** You're asked to appear in an advert with Michael Jackson. Great! But, rats, it's for Nescafé — completely naff. Miss a turn.

**50.** Your single goes into the charts at no. 38 and is featured on Top of the Pops Breakers. Things are lookin' good. Move forward 2 spaces.

**53.** Jazzie B asks you to be the guest singer on Soul II Soul's next release. You are happenin'! Go forward 3.

**54.** Whitney's cousin turns out to be Whitney's twelfth cousin sixteen times removed and doesn't know her at all. Go back 2 spaces.

**57.** George phones you up again but you're too busy to go out with him. Go back 1.

**58.** Someone called Jason sends you an enormous bunch of red roses. But you don't know anyone called Jason, do you? Oh, dear. You must throw a 6 before you can re-start.

**63.** Your single is this week's fastest riser — going up an amazing 24 places to No. 14. TOTP is beckoning. Have another turn.

**65.** You get your hair permed so that it's fab 'n' funky like Neneh Cherry's. You look brilliant. Move on 1.

**69.** You meet Kylie whilst out shopping and she helps you choose some groovy new gear. What a hip chick! Move forward 2.

**70.** You get the call to appear on Top Of The Pops. Move on 5 spaces.

**73.** Deacon Blue ask you to play support for them on their next tour. You don't like them but they play to huge crowds. Oh, trauma — what d'you do? Miss a turn while you decide.

**74.** You're asked to appear on Wogan — but alas, old Terry doesn't want to chat to you, you're only getting to sing. Not really good enough, is it? Move back 3.

**79.** You have a clothes crisis and can't decide what to wear for your grand entrance on TOTP. The result is you're half an hour late on set and lots of peeps are v. cheesed off! Throw a 2 before you start again.

**80.** You meet Paula Abdul on the TOTP set and she gives you a quick dance lesson so that you don't prat about on stage. Move on 1.

**83.** You're pipped to the no. 1 spot by Craig McLachlan. Rats! Go back 5.

**86.** You wake up to discover all your hair's fallen out during the night and you have to take time out to go and get a wig. Miss 2 turns while you're at the shops.

**88.** Your second single is released. Go forward 3 spaces.

# A BE...

**91.** Gloria Estefan invites you round to her swank pad for tea and biscuits. You don't like tea, but you go anyway. Move on 1 space.

**93.** Your publicity officer phones you up and asks you to do an interview with Naffo Newspapers. You tell her to tell them to bog off and you get the reputation of being 'difficult'. Go back one.

**96.** You meet Betty Boo at a showbiz bash and get on like a house on fire. She asks you to work with her on her next single. Have another turn.

**99.** Oh, dear. Your second single was a complete flop and can be found in the bargain bin at Woolies selling for the miserly sum of 10p. And, if this isn't enough, you haven't received a penny from Rip-off Records. You are truly 'Down The Dumper'. Sorry!

**100.** You are a *star!* Your second single's shifting by the truckload, you're coining in the cash and everyone loves you. Congratulations!

# WEIRD OR WHAT?

**So you think *you're* superstitious? Huh! Touching wood is nothing! Take a look at the lengths *some* people used to go to.**

## APPLES

You've all heard the superstition that if you peel an apple in one long strip and chuck the peel over your shoulder, it'll land in the shape of the initial of your future hubby. But have you heard the one about gals who used to stick apple pips to their cheeks, giving each pip the name of a possible heart-throb? Whichever named pip stayed put longest would decide the guy she was going to marry! Sigh . . . if only!

## BEETLES

A black beetle running across the floor of a room was once considered unlucky. And it's even unluckier to kill one — maybe they mean it's unlucky for the beetle, eh? Supposedly, it'll rain heavily for a week if you kill a beetle — obviously a lot of people in Britain have stamped on a beetle or ten.

## CLOVER

Yes, you've all heard that a four-leafed clover is very lucky — and practically impossible to find, too! But did you know that if you wear a four-leafed clover in your right shoe, the first bloke you come across will be your future hubby? Bit risky this one — what if the first guy you bump into happens to be Spotty Sylvester?

## DOCTOR

Before the N.H.S. when you had to pay after every visit, it was considered unlucky to pay the doctor's bill in full there and then. To do so implied too much confidence in a cure. However gipsies always paid in full, believing that unpaid-for medicine wouldn't work. If your doctor moves to a brand new surgery, make sure you get an appointment pronto. To be the first patient in a new surgery is supposed to be lucky!

## EARRINGS

Here's an odd one. Earrings worn in pierced ears are meant to be good for your eyesight. Well, have you ever seen a punk with five earrings in both ears wearing specs? There you go then! Sailors wore plain gold earrings to protect them from drowning. They've got to be earrings for pierced ears, mind you — none of those screw-on jobs will do the trick. But if you can't swim too well, don't depend on your earrings . . . stick with water wings!

## FINGER-NAILS

Some sailors once believed that cutting their nails at sea when it's calm would provoke a storm. And if a young married woman cut her right hand nails with her left hand, she would supposedly rule her husband. It was once also believed that you shouldn't cut a child's nails before he or she was twelve months old, or they would grow up to be light-fingered. Instead, the mother would bite their nails off — *yeuch*! In Wales, it was once thought that burying a child's first nail clipping under an ash tree would make them grow up to be a top singer. Hmmm!

## GLOVES

If you drop your gloves, let someone else pick them up for you — then wait for a pleasant surprise. And if you leave your gloves at a mate's house and go back to get them, sit down before you pick them up and stand up when you put them on. If you don't, you won't be invited back to your mate's house again — or so they used to say!

## HOLLY

Holly is meant to be very lucky and people used to keep a sprig of it aside when they destroyed the rest of their Crimbo decorations — the holly sprig would then protect their house from thunder and lightning the following year. Some girls used to go out at midnight on a Friday, gather nine 'female' holly leaves (the smoother ones, not the sharp prickly ones) and tie them with nine knots (?) in a three-cornered (??) handkerchief. They'd lay this under their pillow and the man they were to marry would appear in their dream that night. It would only work as long as the girl spoke to no one between midnight and dawn.

## IVY

Here we go again — more future hubby superstitions. Ivy was used in a similar way as a four-leafed clover. If a girl carried an ivy leaf in her pocket, the first man she met while out walking would be her future husband . . . even if he was already married! In some places at Hallowe'en, ivy leaves were thrown in pairs on to a fire (a pointed leaf for the bloke and a rounded one for the girl). If the leaves jumped together, the people they represented would marry but if they jumped apart, the relationship would end with a quarrel.

## LADDER

How many of you avoid walking under ladders? Quite a few, we bet. Well, if you accidentally walk under one here's what to do to stop bad luck. Keep your fingers crossed until you see a dog or remain silent until you see a four-legged animal. Other charms are that you make a cross on your shoe with a licked finger and don't look back until the wet mark has disappeared. Then again, you can always shrug and just hope a paint pot doesn't land on your head!

## MOON

A new moon is supposed to be lucky in many ways — but don't point at the moon as this is meant to be unlucky. When the new moon was seen for the first time, people greeted it with a bow or curtsey. In Shropshire, people used to bow nine times to a new moon, making a wish as they did so and turning round between bows. Turning over the silver in your pockets when you see a new moon is meant to be lucky — this should ensure you have plenty dosh for the next month.

## NAILS

If you find a nail lying on the road and pick it up, it's very lucky — especially if the nail is rusty. Once upon a time, when someone was suspected of witchcraft, his or her innocence would be proven by secretly driving a nail into his or her footprint. If the person was a witch they'd be compelled to find the nail and pull it out. If the person wasn't a witch, they'd carry on as normal, unaware of the test. I suppose this was one occasion when picking up a nail from the road wasn't so lucky, eh?

## ONIONS

Girls used to take as many onions as the number of guys they fancied and scratch the name of each one on the various onions. Whichever onion sprouted first would be the one for her. Onions were also used as a cure for chilblains. People rubbed their chilblains with raw onion and salt and hey presto! — their chilblains would be gone. For earache, a roasted onion held against the ear while still hot was meant to be a cure. Yeuch! And yeuchier still, a remedy for baldness was to rub a raw onion over the bald patch until the skin was red. Then honey would be smeared over the bald patch and . . . you'd end up stinking of onions and honey, we suppose!

## PORPOISE

Sailors regarded porpoises as lucky creatures which must never be harmed. Porpoises are said to keep sharks away and if they accompany or play around a ship at sea it is a sign of a good voyage. Porpoises were also believed to control the wind. Their jumping is thought to foretell a storm, but if they play about wildly during a storm, calm weather will supposedly soon follow.

## ROSES

Aaargh! Yet *more* future hubby stuff. If a girl wanted to know who she'd marry, she would pick a rosebud on Midsummers Day, wrap it in white paper and hide it away until Christmas Day. If it was found as fresh as ever, she would wear it to church and hope for the man destined to be her hubby to take it from her. If however, the rosebud had faded and turned brown by Christmas Day, the charm had failed.

## SPIDERS

Spiders are lucky and that's official . . . well, according to superstition anyway! Shiver! A spider in the house is a sign of happiness and security. If one drops from the roof of a house, the owner will receive money. And a money spider running over clothes while they're being worn, means the clothes will soon be replaced by new ones. So next time you want a new outfit sit beside a money spider and hope it crawls over you. Yikes! Is it worth the terror we ask?

## TAXI-CAB NUMBERS

Some taxi drivers believe it is lucky for the index numbers of their cabs to contain a seven or multiples of seven. It's also lucky if their index number contains a letter 'U' because this looks like a horseshoe.

## UMBRELLA

You all know that it's supposed to be unlucky to open an umbrella indoors and hold it above your head. But did you know that it was once considered unlucky to dump your brolly on a bed and that if you open an umbrella on a fine day, it'll rain? Like gloves, if you drop an umbrella, hope there's someone else there to pick it up for you — or prepare to stand and get soaked until someone comes along!

## VIOLETS

In some country districts, it was thought unlucky to bring *less* than a handful of wild violets indoors at a time. To dream about violets is lucky, meaning a change for the better in the dreamer's life. Violets were one of the more pleasant ingredients used in remedies for illnesses which don't exist any more — we won't talk about snails, toads, mice, spide . . . (Cut! The Ed!).

## WHISTLING

Sailors, miners and theatre peeps hate whistling. Sailors feel whistling is like imitating the wind and by doing so they would be magically raising a storm. Miners didn't like whistling because at one time they thought it would annoy The Knockers — the spirits who inhabited the Cornish tin mines. If you whistle in a theatre dressing room, you'll be told to leave the room at once and turn around three times before coming in again.

## YARROW

This is a plant which used to be called Nose-bleed because it was once used to stop nose-bleeds. It was also used to *start* nose-bleeds by sticking a leaf up your nostril — this was meant to ease migraine pains! We recommend you stick to aspirin. Some girls used to stick a yarrow leaf up their nostrils and twist them around as they said a little verse. If their nose bled, the bloke they fancied felt the same. If he didn't fancy her, her nose wouldn't bleed. Well, would you fancy someone who had leaves up their nostrils?

**Well, as you can see, there's more to superstition than crossing your fingers and touching wood. Superstitious people certainly went to weird and wonderful lengths. As for the love superstitions, we recommend you just get your best friend to tell that hunk you fancy him — who wants onions sprouting in their bedroom . . . or leaves sprouting from their nostrils?**

# THE WRONG GUY!

HUH! THAT EXPLAINS IT! WELL, TOO BAD! I'M SURE GREG LIKES ME AND IT'S ONLY A MATTER OF TIME UNTIL HE ASKS ME OUT.
MAYBE KATE'S PARTY THIS SATURDAY'LL BE YOUR BIG CHANCE.
But on Saturday—
HI, YOU TWO — YOU'RE LATE! EVERYONE ELSE HAS BEEN HERE FOR AGES.
WE HAD TO WAIT FOR THE BABYSITTER TO ARRIVE AND LOOK AFTER MY LITTLE BROTHER. MUM AND DAD HAVE GONE OUT TONIGHT, TOO.
I JUST HOPE LUCY HASN'T HAD TIME TO GET HER CLAWS INTO GREG.
OH, NO! IT LOOKS AS IF I JUST HAVE TO ADMIT DEFEAT. IT'D TAKE A CROW-BAR TO PRISE THOSE TWO APART.
I WAS BEGINNING TO THINK YOU WEREN'T COMING, AVRIL. HOW ABOUT A DANCE?
OKAY, SEAN.
I'M SURPRISED SEAN'S BOTHERING WITH ME. THERE'S NO NEED, NOW THAT DONNA'S GOT GREG WELL AND TRULY IN HER CLUTCHES.
OH, WELL! I MAY AS WELL TRY TO ENJOY MYSELF. SEAN'S NOT BAD-LOOKING, EVEN ALTHOUGH HE ISN'T THE RIGHT GUY.
After the party—
I'M GOING YOUR WAY SO I'LL WALK YOU HOME IF YOU LIKE, AVRIL.
THANKS, SEAN — THAT'D BE NICE.

And—
WOW! I — I WASN'T EXPECTING THIS!
But, on Monday morning—
THERE'S GREG ON HIS OWN — AND SEAN'S NOWHERE IN SIGHT. NOW'S MY CHANCE!
HI, GREG. DID YOU ENJOY THE PARTY ON SATURDAY?
IT WAS OKAY. PITY ABOUT THE SOUND SYSTEM, THOUGH. IT WAS REALLY LOUSY. I'VE GOT A BRILLIANT ONE AT HOME.
OH — REALLY? WELL, ER, DID YOU MANAGE TO DO ANY REVISION FOR THE FRENCH TEST TODAY?
NOT MUCH — BUT I'M NOT ALL THAT WORRIED. I DON'T HAVE ANY PROBLEMS WITH LANGUAGES.
SEE YOU, AVRIL. I'D BETTER GO — I CAN SEE ONE OF MY FANS WAITING!
HUH! SO THAT'S WHAT HE THINKS OF LUCY! I THOUGHT I'D ENVY HER — BUT INSTEAD, I FEEL SORRY FOR HER.
And—
HI, AVRIL. THERE'S — ER — SOMETHING I HAVE TO TELL YOU.
IF IT'S ABOUT YOU HELPING YOUR COUSIN, SEAN, THEN I ALREADY KNOW.
YOU DO? OH, I SEE. BUT THE THING IS I REALLY LIKE YOU, AVRIL. WOULD — WOULD YOU COME OUT WITH ME SOME TIME?
YES, SEAN — I'D LOVE THAT.
AND I REALLY WOULD! LOOKS LIKE THE WRONG GUY'S TURNED OUT TO BE THE RIGHT GUY AFTER ALL!
THE END

# I RESOLVE...

## ... to keep all these resolutions to make 1992 my most beautiful yet!

### HAIR

... to give my hair a new lease of life by investing in a good cut.
... to talk to my hairdresser before I decide to do anything drastic — he or she will know the best style to suit my appearance and lifestyle.
... to condition my hair well after swimming.
... to pay attention to my diet. A bad diet will soon show up in the condition of my hair.
... to make sure my hair's trimmed regularly — even if I'm growing it.

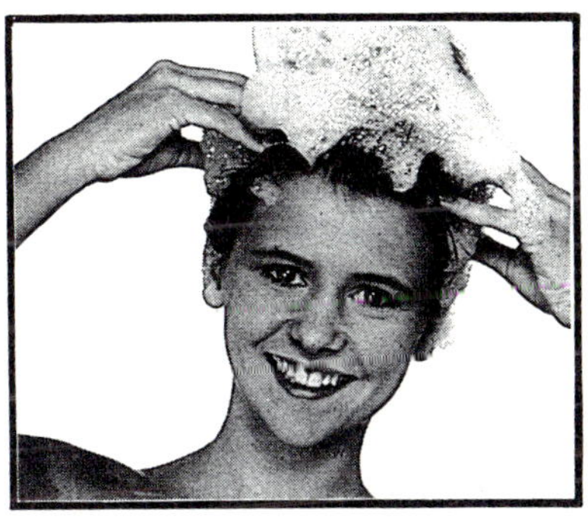

### TEETH

... to greet the new year with a sparkling smile.
... to brush my teeth for at least five minutes every day.
... to invest in dental floss to make sure the surfaces in between my teeth aren't neglected.
... to change my toothbrush every two to three months.
... to visit my dentist regularly — whether I'm in pain or not.
... to brush my teeth thoroughly after eating sweets.
... to chew dental gum, a hunk of cheese or some raw carrot after eating sweets if I can't brush my teeth to rid my mouth of the harmful acids that can cause tooth decay.

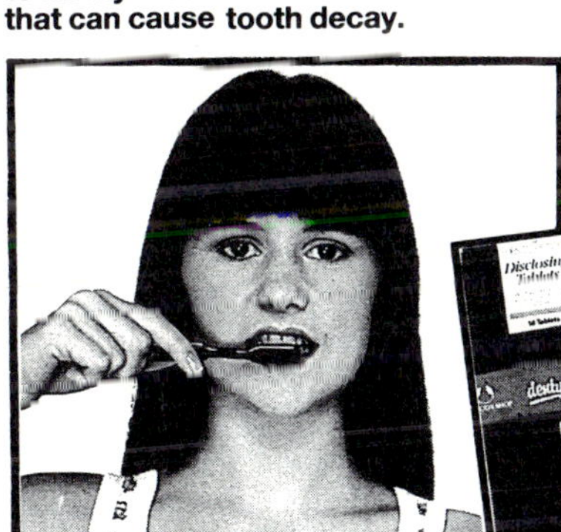

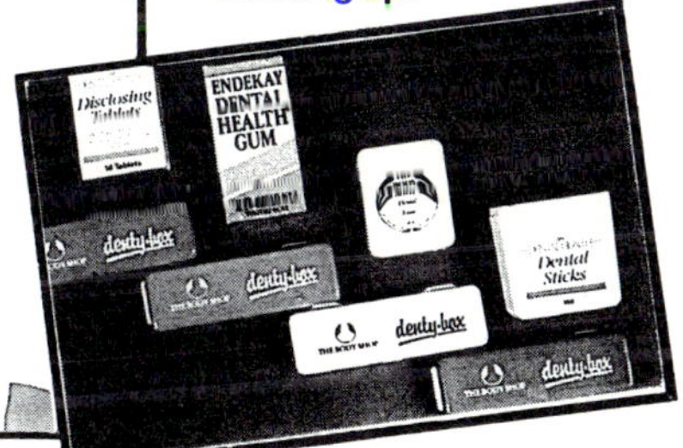

### SKIN

... to treat my skin more kindly.
... to try not to linger more than fifteen minutes in my bath, so that my skin won't start to wrinkle and lose natural oils.
... to swap hot baths for cool showers. They'll boost my circulation and make me wake up in the morning.
... to moisturise my skin well after my bath or shower. I know my skin needs help to stay soft and smooth in winter.

### NAILS

... not to bite my nails.
... to give myself a manicure to discourage me from nibbling.
... to keep my hands busy — this will help my nails to grow *and* stop them straying to my mouth.
... not to wear coloured varnish all the time — I know it can stain my nails.
... to protect my hands and nails by wearing rubber gloves when I do the washing up.

### SMOKING

... to stop smoking if I've been stupid enough to start. It ruins my health and appearance, makes me smell *and* costs a fortune.
... to never be tempted to start if I've never smoked.
... to write to ASH (Action on Smoking and Health), 5-11 Mortimer Street, London if I need help and advice on how to stop smoking.

### BODY

... to exercise regularly. It'll make me fit and cheer me up — people who exercise are generally happier than those who don't.
... to check out the feature on pages 60 + 61 to find out which sport is best for me.
... to remember it's important to warm up properly before I start to exercise.
... to stop exercising if I feel faint, short of breath or develop cramp.
... to stick to my exercise routine once I've found one that suits me.

## ... to try to keep all my resolutions for as long as poss. I know they'll be worth it!

continued from page 56.

# too old!

## PART THREE

WE'LL ALL BE TALKING ABOUT THE FANCY DRESS, ANYWAY, SO YOU WOULDN'T BE INTERESTED.
SEE YOU!
I FEEL SORT OF LEFT OUT. BUT IT'S WORTH IT. TOM REALLY **IS** SPECIAL!
Then —
HI, LYNN!
OH! TOM'S WITH A COUPLE OF HIS CLASSMATES. I THOUGHT IT WAS JUST GOING TO BE HIM AND ME.
SARA AND DAN HAVE DECIDED TO COME ALONG TOO. YOU'LL LIKE THEM.
I FEEL DEAD NERVOUS. WHAT IF THEY TREAT ME LIKE SOME SILLY KID?
I REMEMBER THAT SOLO YOU SANG AT THE SCHOOL CONCERT. DAN AND I ARE KEEN ON MUSIC, TOO.
DID YOU HEAR THE BACH RECITAL ON TV LAST NIGHT?
WASN'T IT BRILLIANT?
OH, NO! JUST 'COS I SING, THEY THINK I'M INTO CLASSICAL MUSIC! THE TRUTH IS I CAN'T **STAND** IT!

continued on page 98.

# ONLY MAKE-BELIEVE...

I WAS really nervous about moving to a new town, especially at the beginning of the school holidays. There'd be weeks and weeks until I started school . . . and I wouldn't know a soul.

But the first evening, as I helped Mum hang curtains, I saw several girls my age congregate on a piece of grass outside our house. All I needed to do was to pluck up the courage to speak to them. Then I'd have some friends.

It sounded easy, but it was really nerve-racking going over to speak to them the first time. I was scared they'd tell me to get lost. But they didn't! They seemed really friendly. I was soon telling them all about myself — and learning lots about them, too.

And that's when the problem started, because I soon realised that every single one of them had a boyfriend. And me? Well, I'd never been out with a boy in my life!

I really panicked as I heard them talking about the places their boyfriends had taken them and the things they'd said to each other. They sounded so grown up!

I was sure they'd soon get tired of *me* when they found I couldn't join in. If only I had a boyfriend, too.

That's when I had my idea. I didn't really have a boyfriend — but they didn't ever have to find out. I could pretend that I *did*.

Because I'd just moved from a town miles away, it was easy. I told my new friends that I'd been going out with a boy called Graham for months.

They fell for it completely! Soon they were asking me all kinds of questions about him — what he looked like, if we'd been at the same school, how close he'd lived to me, and so on. I was the centre of attention.

It was great being part of the gang. They showed me round the town and they introduced me to lots of other people. There was Mrs Watson who had several young children and was often looking for a babysitter. She paid well and the girls said I could get a turn too. And then there was hunky Richard who lived at the end of the road. He was really great. I wished he was my *real* boyfriend. It'd be a lot better fun than just having a make-believe one.

The next few weeks passed quickly. Most evenings I met the girls. Sometimes one of them was missing because she'd gone out with her boyfriend, and sometimes they all had dates and I was left completely alone. I spent these evenings writing letters. My mates all imagined I was writing to Graham, but actually I was writing pretend letters from him to me — so that I could show them to my friends and make my story seem more real. I thought I was being really clever.

Then, suddenly, something amazing happened. Richard asked me out!

He stopped me when I was walking down the street alone and asked me to go to the pictures. I was flabbergasted — and delighted. Now I'd have a real live boyfriend to talk about and not just a make-believe one.

I was about to tell Richard that I'd love to go out with him, when Mary — one of my new mates — came along.

"What are you two talking about?" she asked casually.

"I've just asked Suzy out," Richard explained. "What do you say, Suzy?"

But before I got the chance to say anything, Mary spoke up.

"Suzy can't go out with you, Richard!" she said. "She already has a boyfriend called Graham. He lives in her old town."

I couldn't do anything but agree. I was so disappointed! If only Mary hadn't come along when she did. But I knew it wasn't really her fault. It was mine. I shouldn't have told all those lies.

And then, a few days later, I realised that all my lies had been for nothing anyway. One of the other girls in the gang, Alison, was chucked by her boyfriend. She was all on her own — like I'd been when I first arrived. But she wasn't cut out because of it. The others liked her whether she had a boyfriend or not. And they'd have liked me too — I was sure now. All my lies had been for nothing.

But because I invented a make-believe boyfriend, I lost the chance of a date with a real live guy.

What a fool I'd been! What a fool!

# SCROOGE

**Could you have added another twenty tips to Scrooge's guide on page 49 . . . or does stinginess not exist in your books? Find out if you're a Scrooge or a Santa with our personality quiz.**

**1. Have you ever given one of the Crimbo presents you received to someone else the following year?**
a) No way! That'd be a rotten thing to do. It's not on!
b) You've thought about it, but it'd be dead embarrassing if you gave it back to the person who'd given it to you in the first place.
c) Yeah! Well, it's as well going to someone who'll like it. Waste not, want not.

**2. Your best mate's been sick and she's in bed, feeling down in the dumps. Do you —**
b) Pay her a visit and give her all the latest gossip?
c) Phone her with a note of the chapters she's missed in Geography and German?
a) Buy her some of her fave mags and sweets, and take her some of your records to play?

**3. You don't have enough money for the disco *and* your mum's Christmas pressie. Do you —**
c) Go to the disco and worry about Mum's pressie another day?
b) Ask Dad for a sub on your pocket money?
a) Do lots of odd jobs for Dad to earn some extra dosh?

**4. What do you look for in the record shop?**
a) Something your mates will enjoy, too, when they come round to your house.
b) Your fave album even though your mates hate it. It's *you* who's going to be listening to it, after all.
c) Some ace bargains in the reduced section — even though you've never heard of most of them.

**5. A classmate is having a Crimbo party. Everyone's invited and everyone's to bring some nibbles. Do you —**
c) Turn up empty-handed with an excuse about your dog nicking off with the cake you'd bought?
a) Look up a cookery book and spend ages making something really festive and tasty?
b) Buy a couple of bags of nuts and crisps?

**6. How much money have you got at the moment?**
a) A few pounds here and there, and a few more that you've lent friends here and there.
c) Five pounds in your piggy bank, three pounds, twenty pence in your change bottle and twenty odd pounds in a building society.
b) About a fiver in your piggy bank — you're not that sure really.

**7. You're shopping with a mate and she sees a great top that's a snip at a tenner. But she's only got seven squids on her. Do you —**
a) Insist on lending her the three quid. You can do without that top *you* fancied?
c) Sympathise a bit, but if she can't save her money for a rainy day, that's her hard cheese?
b) Offer to lend her the three quid at the end of the day if you haven't spent it?

**8. The school are having a jumble sale. What do you do to help?**
c) Offer your services behind a stall. That way you'll be too busy to waste your money at the other stalls.
b) Clear out the things in your attic and a few things in your room that you can't stand.
a) Collect together all the things in your room which you don't really use any more — even though you still like them a bit.

# OR SANTA?

**13. That guy you fancy has asked you to go to the cinema — but you know he doesn't have a lot of dosh. Do you —**

c) Treat it as one of your normal dates and let him pay for everything?
b) Let him pay you in — but buy him a hot dog in return?
a) Insist on going dutch. Why should the guy always have to pay? In fact, you might even offer to pay *him* in?

**14. What's your fave part of the festive season?**

a) Hanging decorations, organising rave-ups and Christmas shopping.
b) Opening your pressies, Christmas dinner, and going to parties.
c) Counting the cash you've been given and looking forward to the January sales.

**9. The youth club Crimbo party is going to be fancy dress. Do you —**

b) Rummage though your aunt's wardrobe for some sixties gear?
a) Spend ages making outfits for you *and* your mates?
c) Decide not to go. You don't have the time or the dosh to waste on a costume for a daft fancy dress party?

**10. A mate borrows your new skirt for a disco. Disaster strikes and she splits your skirt right up the back seam. Do you —**

a) Get busy with the sewing machine — it's only the seam after all?
c) Give her a good yelling at. Honestly, some people have no respect for other folk's property?
b) Ask her to mend it. And think carefully next time about lending her your clothes if you think they're too small for her?

**11. What do you think of fairgrounds ?**

b) They're good fun and they make a change from the disco.
c) They're a swindle. Fifty pence for three minutes' ride — stuff that!
a) They're totally brilliant fun. You wish they'd come to your town every week.

**12. Do you buy "Hi!" every week?**

a) Yes — and you finally get to read it when your family and friends have finished with it.
c) No — you read it in the newsagent's or nick it from your friend.
b) Yes — but no one gets their hands on it till you've finished it and taken out the pin-ups you want.

## conclusions

**mostly a's**

You are definitely a soft-hearted Santa. You love all the Christmas festivities, organising parties and having fun with your friends. If your friends aren't enjoying themselves, you won't feel happy either. But sometimes you're too generous for your own good. You *are* allowed to say 'no' sometimes when you can't help, you know. Be careful not to be taken for a sucker. Think about yourself a bit more.

**mostly b's**

You've got the balance just right. You enjoy Christmas and partying as much as the next person. And you're willing to help friends whenever you can but on your conditions — you won't let them walk all over you. You're not a sucker, but you're definitely far from being a stingy Scrooge.

**mostly c's**

Do you know what Christmas is? Well, it's a good excuse for partying and enjoying yourself for one thing, in case you didn't know. Loosen up a bit! There's nothing wrong with being careful about your money, but you're taking it too far. Does everything have to come down to how much you can save or spend on you, you?

# The Hi! Soap The Valley Girls

THERE'S A YOUTH CLUB ON TONIGHT. WANT TO GO, DORRIE?
YEAH. YOU'RE LUCKY HERE ON THE VALLEY. I LIVE OUT IN THE WILDS AND WE HAVE TO TRAVEL MILES TO FIND ANY LIFE!
So —
HI, GIRLS. DO — EM — YOU TWO WANT TO JOIN ME AND EDDIE FOR TABLE TENNIS?
TYPICAL — I'VE FANCIED MIKE MAXTON FOR AGES AND NOW HE MAKES A MOVE ON MY GOOD-LOOKING COUSIN!
But, after the game —
ER — I GOT YOU A COKE, LINDA.
OH! TH-THANKS, MIKE!
HAR! HAR! METHINKS YOU'VE GOT AN ADMIRER THERE, COUSIN!
OH, GIVE OVER, DORRIE!
Next day —
WHAT'S WITH YOUR LITTLE BRUV, ZOE?
HE'S IN LURVE, KAY. HE'S BEEN LIKE THAT EVER SINCE HE SET EYES ON DORRIE.
POOR DAVID . . . HE'S PROBABLY TOO SHY TO TALK TO HER.
Later —
I'VE WRITTEN TO DORRIE — A SECRET NOTE. I COULDN'T ASK HER OUT FACE TO FACE! NO WAY.
MEET ME AT MAC DONALD'S TONIGHT, 7.30 - I'LL BE WEARING A BLUE JACKET. - AN ADMIRER!
But David hadn't put Dorrie's name on the front!
WHAT'S THIS? "AN ADMIRER" — IT'S GOT TO BE FROM MIKE! IMAGINE HIM WANTING TO DATE ME!

Later —
WHICH LIPSTICK — PINK OR DARK RED? I WANT TO LOOK MY BEST FOR MIKE. IMAGINE SENDING A NOTE. HE'S SO ROMANTIC!
I HOPE I KNOW WHAT TO SAY TO DORRIE. IF SHE TURNS UP IN THE FIRST PLACE! I FEEL REALLY NERVOUS!
HEY, WHAT'RE YOU ALL POSHED UP FOR?
IF YOU MUST KNOW — I'M GOING TO MEET SOMEONE SPECIAL!
WHOA! DON'T TELL ME — DORRIE!
YEAH. I SENT HER A MYSTERY NOTE. SHE WON'T BE ABLE TO RESIST TURNING UP AT MACDONALD'S TO SEE WHO I AM!
So —
HEY, MY DOZY BRUV'S SET UP A MYSTERY DATE WITH DORRIE! WANT TO GO ALONG AND SEE THE FUN?
OH, ZOE, WHAT AN AWFUL THING TO DO!
YEAH, TERRIBLE! COUNT ME IN! LET'S PHONE TO SEE IF LINDA WANTS TO COME TOO.
NO ANSWER. OH, WELL — SHE MUST BE OUT.
Kay, Zoe and Bev hurried to Macdonald's —
THERE'S LOVER BOY. MAKE SURE HE DOESN'T SEE US!
WONDER IF SHE'LL TURN UP, OR IF SHE'S SUSSED HIM?
HOPE SHE COMES . . . THIS IS KILLING ME!
CRIKEY! LOOK WHO'S COMING! I DON'T BELIEVE IT!

LINDA!
YOU!
OH, CRIKEY! I — MEANT . . .
AND I THOUGHT . . . OH, DEAR! HA, HA, HA!
Then —
HA! HA! WHAT A LAUGH!
WHAT THE . . . YOU ROTTEN LOT! YOU WERE SPYING ON ME!
WE WEREN'T SPYING ON YOU, LIN. WE WERE SPYING ON LOVER BOY THERE!
SORRY ABOUT THE MIX UP, LIN. I — UM — SENT THAT NOTE TO . . .
DORRIE! SHE WAS OUT ALL AFTERNOON. I TELL YOU WHAT — I'LL PUT IN A GOOD WORD FOR YOU.
YOU CAN DO IT NOW!
DORRIE!
I FOUND THE NOTE ON YOUR BED, LIN, AND I THOUGHT IT MUST BE FROM MIKE, SO I CAME ALONG TO SEE THE FUN! BUT NOW I'M HERE . . . LIKE TO BUY ME A BURGER, DAVID?
RIGHT, YOU LOT — PUSH OFF!
GUESS WHAT, LIN? ON OUR WAY HERE, WE PASSED MIKE IN THE PARK.
LET'S GO!
THE END

# AAAAAAAGHH!

## how to stay sane at Christmas!

**Hibernate!**

Stick a smiley mask to your face!

**Persuade your parents to take you all off to some remote foreign land where they've never even HEARD of Christmas, using the money they'd just 'waste' if they stayed at home.**

Invent an anti-"wimp with mistletoe detector" and USE it!

**Practise saying "It's absolutely LOVELY — just what I've always wanted!" wearing a huge grin, in your mirror every night for at least 6 months before the dreaded season.**

Bribe someone else into doing everything for you!

**Run off your "vague, but covering EVERY possibility" thank you letters, well in advance.**

Keep clear of the kitchen! If something goes wrong, it'll be YOUR fault!

**Perfect your Monopoly cheating technique so you won't cry when Grandad beats you yet again!**

Make sure your brother's well versed when your parents ask him what records you'd like for Christmas. Let him know that if he says Chris De Burgh, he's dead!

**Give everyone EXACTLY the same pressie, wrapped in exactly the same paper — peasy!**

Better still, give 'em gift tokens!

**Or, inform them a donation to charity has been made on their behalf!**

Tell your little bruv or sis that Santa won't come unless he or she is VERY quiet for a VERY long time! (Two weeks? A Month? It's up to you!)

**Go to the other extreme! Have all your pressies bought and wrapped by Easter AND remember where you hid them.**

Develop a mysterious disease which won't hurt but will leave you confined to bed for at least a month. (Two weeks BEFORE and two weeks AFTER Christmas!)

**Wrap yourself up with a hamper in a box bearing the label, "Do not open until March 3rd"!**

Stick your Christmas stocking over your little bruv's head to keep him quiet.

**Throw yourself into the festivities with a vengeance. Help with absolutely everything. When you conk out with exhaustion, you'll be too tired to care!**

Grin and bear it! Why should YOU be any different?

# DO YOU ALWAYS TELL THE TRUTH

**We have ways of finding out, you know! One of which is to answer this quiz, but remember — you do so at your peril!**

**1. You're late for school *again*. When asked why, you . . .**
a. Admit you were far too snug in your cosy little bed to risk diving out a second sooner than necessary.
b. Explain a few passing Martians asked you the way to Woolworths and you thought you'd better tell them in case they did something awful to this lovely little planet.
c. Insist you were halfway to school when you remembered your History project just *had* to be handed in, so you trotted back off home for it.

**2. You and the dog have been left in the same room as a very tempting box of chocolates. 'Mysteriously', a few go missing. Your mum calls upon you to explain. Do you . . .**
a. Think about pretending it was the dog, feel incredibly guilty and finally admit that you "only had *one*!"
b. Shout excitedly, "Isn't it amazing! We've got the only dog in the world addicted to coffee creams!"
c. Say "Not me!" but look *very* pointedly at your trusty mutt.

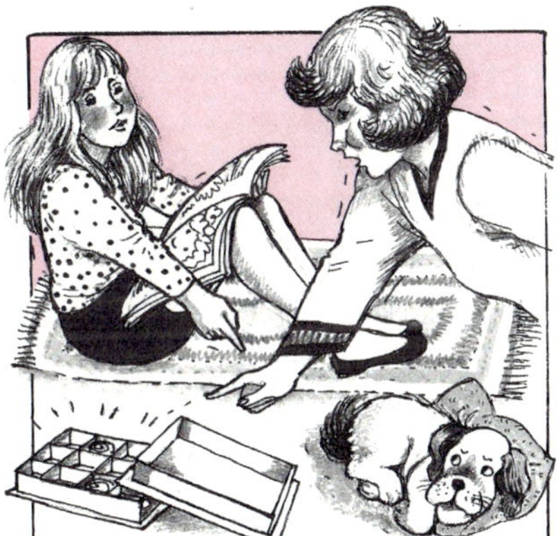

**3. The boy of your dreams asks if you're interested in stamp collecting. You reply . . .**
a. "Um . . . not really . . . sorry . . ."
b. "How did you guess? I've saved every stamp from every letter I've ever received!", peering at him earnestly through your giant-sized magnifying glass.
c. "Well, yeah, I used to be, till my dog/cat/little bruv ruined my collection."

**4. "You were told to be home at 9.30 pm. It's now 10.05 pm. Why?" Your very angry mum is awaiting an explanation. What's your story?**
a. "You wouldn't *believe* how many punctures Mr Simpson had, Mum, honest!"
b. "I forgot the time. I'm sorry."
c. "We had to drop off Sandra and Tracey first . . ."

**5. Your sister comes home from the hairdresser's with a perm. It's awful. She asks what you think — what you *really* think. What do you say?**
a. "It's lovely! It really suits you."
b. "It looks a bit new. I'm sure it'll be super when it settles down."
c. "It's awful! You look like a Brillo pad!"

**6. The maths teacher sends you to collect something from the boot of his car. When you open the boot you find the questions for your class's next exam scribbled on a bit of paper. What do you do?**
a. Own up that you saw them and, although you didn't read them, of course, suggest he sets a new exam?
b. Have a quick read. It'll be nice to pass Maths for a change.
c. Shut the boot without reading the questions and say nothing?

**7. Your gran offers you an ornament that belonged to her gran. It's a family heirloom, Gran says, and worth a bit. But you *hate* it. What do you do?**
a. You take it and put it in a drawer, only bringing it out when Gran comes to visit. After all, you don't like to hurt her feelings and if it is worth something, well . . .
b. You tell Gran you feel you're too young to appreciate the ornament yet. Anyway, you think she shouldn't part with something that means so much to her.
c. You tell Gran you've always loved the ornament and you'll treasure it forever.

**8. Your cousin comes to visit with her new baby (a real ugly bug) and proudly asks if he isn't the most beautiful baby you've ever seen. Do you . . .**
a. Lie through your teeth and agree with her.
b. Say something like, "He's certainly a happy baby, anyway!"
c. Be completely honest and cause the biggest family feud of the century.

**9. Your teacher is convinced she saw you sneaking off home last Tuesday when you should have been cross-country running. Well, did she?**
a. "Um . . . yes, Miss. Sorry, Miss, but my friend *made* me, Miss . . ."
b. Yup, but you were on your way to the . . . um . . . dentist.
c. Certainly not! You love cross-country running. It's your life! In fact, you want to be put in the team — right this very minute!

**10. A girl in your class fancies your older brother but he can't stand her. When she gets a Valentine from a boy she doesn't know, she thinks it's him and asks you to take one back to him. What do you do?**
a. Try to tell her that perhaps she has more than one admirer and she shouldn't jump to conclusions.
b. Take it home and say nothing. After all, it's none of your business.
c. Tell her your brother didn't send her card. He's too stingy to send Valentines.

## SCORES

| | | | |
|---|---|---|---|
| 1. | a) 1 | b) 3 | c) 2 |
| 2. | a) 1 | b) 3 | c) 2 |
| 3. | a) 1 | b) 3 | c) 2 |
| 4. | a) 3 | b) 1 | c) 2 |
| 5. | a) 3 | b) 2 | c) 1 |
| 6. | a) 1 | b) 3 | c) 2 |
| 7. | a) 1 | b) 2 | c) 3 |
| 8. | a) 3 | b) 2 | c) 1 |
| 9. | a) 1 | b) 2 | c) 3 |
| 10. | a) 3 | b) 2 | c) 1 |

## CONCLUSIONS

**0-13**
Honest to a fault, that's you! You can always be relied upon to tell the whole truth and nothing but the truth, no matter how much it's going to hurt the person concerned. People know you'll always tell them exactly what you think but, because the news is unlikely to ever be good, it's unlikely they'll ever bother to ask you.

**14-23**
The biggest fibber of the lot, that's you! Oh, you may not tell the *biggest* lies, but the fibs you do tell are *so* believable you can talk yourself out of the tightest of corners at any time. All your stories are carefully calculated to make people believe you are telling the truth and that the sticky situations you've landed yourself in are not your fault. Tsk! Tsk!

**Over 24**
Bet you thought you'd be classed the biggest fibber of the lot, eh? Well, you're not. You may be the biggest *fool*, if you expect people to fall for your silly stories, but you're really not a very good fibber at all. Stories have got to have some believable thread running through them or *no one* will ever believe you!

# JILL'S

**We know that lots of you have problems with friends, and it's hard because there doesn't seem to be anyone to talk to. But "Hi!" can help . . .**

**My best friend has got a new friend and doesn't want to spend so much time with me. I get really jealous. I don't think they want me around any more.**

It is upsetting when you feel you're being left out — maybe you could explain this to your best friend. It may just be that she wants to be friends with this other girl as well. If she's a real pal, she won't leave you out of things.

**My best friend and I don't seem to get on very well any more.**

As people grow up, they change quite a bit. Perhaps the reason that you don't get on so well any more is that you've both changed in different ways. It is a tricky situation, though, as there isn't any specific problem to point out. Try to keep your friendship going but don't feel tied to each other. Eventually, you'll be able to sort out how you feel. I think you should both feel free to make new friends, though.

**My best friend's started smoking.**

Whatever happens, don't *you* start. Everyone knows the danger of the serious illnesses caused by cigarettes. Tell her how you feel about it and hopefully she'll see sense and stop.

**My best friend's got a boyfriend, but I don't.**

Obviously, she'll want to spend time with him and this could lead to friction between the two of you. Point out that you should still go out together but do try to stay out of their relationship. Remember that, as her best friend, you'll probably still be around long after he's gone! And don't feel jealous — of *course* you'll have a boyfriend too. Just wait and see.

**My friends speak about me behind my back. They tell my secrets and embarrass me in front of people.**

A lot of people don't realise that there's a definite art to being a good friend — and it doesn't sound like these people are doing very well at it. For a start, they're hurting your feelings by making fun of you. Friends should be caring and understanding — and you should be able to have a good laugh *with* them, instead of them laughing at you. Tell them how you feel, and if they don't start treating you better — look for new mates.

**My best friend is moving away.**

Of course you'll promise to keep in contact but there's no denying that it won't be the same. Try to be brave and believe that you *will* make new friends. Keep smiling — getting through a tough time like this means you'll need help from other friends so don't be afraid to share your problem.

# FRIENDS

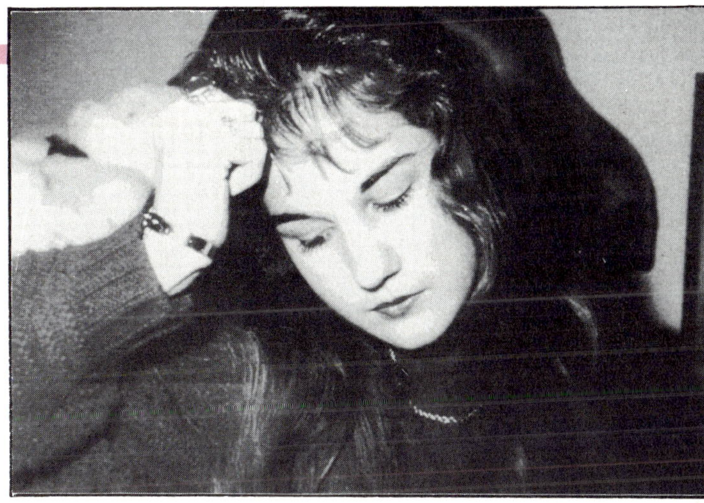

**I don't have any friends.**

Is this because you're shy and don't find it easy to get to know people? Try to relax and be yourself. You don't have anything to prove, you know. Remember that you are just as good a person as anyone else and you'll soon find yourself feeling better. Get involved in clubs in school and outside school so you can meet people with the same interests as yourself. This should be a good start.

**My pal always puts me down. Whenever I do something or get something new, she just slags me off. I never say anything like that to *her*!**

I think the problem here has something to do with jealousy. Believe it or not, your friend is probably acting like this because she's jealous of you. On the other hand, she could have a problem or worry of her own that's upsetting her. Try to understand how she feels.

**My friend keeps copying me — my hairstyle, my clothes, everything I say even! It's really annoying.**

It certainly is annoying when this happens — but, after all, she must think an awful lot of you to want to be so much like you. You could try not talking about new things that you like or want so that you can stay one step ahead of her. Maybe you could try hinting that you always seem to look like twins. Hopefully, she'll soon grow out of this habit.

**My best friend keeps flirting with my boyfriend .**

Are you sure your best friend doesn't flirt with *all* boys? Some girls just seem to flirt all the time! Even so, she should be a bit more considerate as far as your boyfriend's concerned. Hopefully, he won't take much notice of her and it won't affect your relationship. But don't be afraid to mention it to her if this really upsets you.

# CROSSIE TWO!

**Okay, here's *another* crossie to make you even *more* cross! But don't despair — all the answers can be found in the ever-so-wonderful "Hi!" Annual. (What, *all* of them? — The Ed.) Well — er — maybe some of them are a teensie bit of a cheat, sort of!**

## ACROSS

1. You'll find lots of these hunks in the Annual! **(11)**
7. Silly animals do this (x 3)! **(3)**
8. The first photo story. **(2, 6)**
11. Short for the *last* photo story! **(1, 1)**
12. This Adam made someone cringe! **(3)**
17. A little black dress could be this, according to our Fashion Ed! **(3, 5)**
18. A "handy" limb for turning the "Hi!" Annual pages! **(3)**
20. The "Hi!" staff all --- goodie bags from the Ed! **(3)**
22. Who deserves a "Hi!" Annual the most? **(2)**
24. Where you'll find the answers! **(3, 2, 6)**
25. If you're mega-famous, you're this, or you could be on top of a Christmas tree! **(4)**
27. Short for the end! **(1, 1)**
28. It's this animal's life in our "Hi!" love story. **(3)**
29. Page 44 tells you this favourite colour of the fire signs. **(3)**
31. 42 ACROSS, 20 DOWN, 36 DOWN. The four elements of the zodiac. See Sign Up! **(4, 3, 5, 5)**
32. The scene's this colour, and so is grass! **(5)**
34. A ballerina wears this. (What's this got to do with the Annual? — The Ed.). Oops — and so does the Ed to Christmas parties! (Rubbish! — The Ed.) **(4)**
35. Short for desperate — which is what the previous clue is! **(3)**
37. Lots of 25 ACROSS can do this. **(4)**
39. You need two to kiss under the mistletoe! **(3)**
40. You'd be very ----- if you followed the advice on page 49! **(5)**
42. See 31 ACROSS.
43. It's this when you come to the end. **(4)**
44. You could make this pie from a fruit on page 76. **(4)**
46. The only way is up for this ex DJ. **(4)**
47. A "Hi!" Annual is the best pressie on this day! **(9)**

## DOWN

1. This evergreen is very lucky — especially if you're superstitious. **(5)**
2. What you'll say when you read our love story on page 43. (It's also the Ed's initials!) **(1, 1)**
3. 13 DOWN is this in our four-part photo story. **(3, 3)**
4. What to do with your "Hi!" Annual! **(4)**
5. It's green! **(5)**
6. Jackie's mate in "Guilty". **(4)**
9. This shop provided some "old-timers"! **(1, 1)**
10. Bev, Linda, Zoe and Kay. **(3, 6, 5)**
13. Is he "too old", or is he Liz's dreamboat? **(3)**
14. Lots of letters on these pages. **(2, 5)**
15. "Hi!" could be this if it was technical! **(4)**
16. The young girlfriend of 13 DOWN. **(4)**
18. Pages 2 and 3 take place at this time of day! **(1, 1)**
19. Make this to buy *next* year's "Hi!" Annual! And read some more on page 81! **(10)**
20. See 31 ACROSS.
21. Part --- starts on page 17. **(3)**
23. Short for "Hi!" Annual! **(1, 1)**
26. Tom Cruise (our Liz's hero) starred in this abbreviated film. **(1, 1)**
30. The last word on page 119. **(3)**
32. 6 DOWN is in this photo story. **(6)**
33. The big boss lady! **(2)**
36. See 31 ACROSS. **(5)**
37. It's a question of this! **(5)**
38. You'll want to do this when you read page 65! **(3)**
39. Page 12's classic jeans. **(4)**
41. Emilio Estevez is a shortened one of these! **(1, 1)**
45. Another 41 DOWN — bet he'd love pages 22 and 23! **(1, 1)**

**ANSWERS**

**Across: 1.** Heartthrobs, **7.** Say, **8.** No Chance, **11.** Love Letter, **12.** Ant, **17.** Old Timer, **18.** Arm, **20.** Won, **22.** Me, **24.** The Hi! Annual, **25.** Star, **27.** The End, **28.** Dog, **29.** Red, **31.** Fire, **32.** Green, **34.** Tutu, **35.** Des, **37.** Sing, **39.** Lip, **40.** Silly, **42.** Air, **43.** Over, **44.** Tart, **46.** Andy, **47.** Christmas.

**Down: 1.** Holly, **2.** Aw, **3.** Too Old, **4.** Read, **5.** Scene, **6.** Dawn, **9.** C.A., **10.** The Valley Girls, **13.** Tom, **14.** Hi There, **15.** Tech, **16.** Lynn, **18.** a.m., **19.** Resolution, **20.** Water, **21.** One, **23.** Hi Annual, **26.** Top Gun, **30.** End, **32.** Guilty, **33.** Ed, **36.** Earth, **37.** Sport, **38.** Eat, **39.** Levi, **41.** Young American, **45.** River Phoenix.

# THE LUCKY ONE

I ALWAYS envied April Davies — right from the first day she started at our school. I remember the exact moment she arrived. She walked into our classroom and all the boys immediately stopped what they were doing and stared at her. They were totally gobsmacked. And you could see why!

April was a knock out! She was tall and blonde with a great figure and a brilliant tan. And she was always dead trendy!

"Why can't I have clothes like that?" I thought miserably, as I fingered my jacket and plain school skirt. It didn't seem fair!

Clothes weren't the only thing April had plenty of either. She also had every decent record that came out, half a dozen different magazines every week and all the extras like a tennis racquet, sports bag, running shoes, the lot — and all posh makes too.

"Her parents must be loaded!" someone whispered at school one day, as April arrived in yet another new coat.

"They are," somebody else replied. "They live in one of those huge houses in Birch Lane."

I knew Birch Lane well. I walked down it every day to get to school and I'd always admired the big houses with their massive gardens and swanky sports cars on the drive. Trust April to live in one of those, while all I had was a shared bedroom in a tiny terrace, and only a concrete yard for a 'garden'! She was so lucky!

Then I heard that April had a pony — and I envied her even more. I'd always wanted a horse, but I knew there was no chance of me ever getting one.

Naturally enough, April soon had all the boys flocking round her. In fact, she'd only been at our school a week when she landed her first date — and with Gary Summers, too! He was the best looking boy in the third year.

"I've fancied him for months!" I moaned miserably to my mates, when I found out about it.

"Me too," Laura replied. "But he's never looked at any of us."

April and Gary lasted quite a while. But she finished with him when the school holidays came and she went off to the Caribbean for three weeks with her parents.

"I want to have fun on holiday," she explained, "and that means a holiday romance. It wouldn't be fair to Gary though if I was still going out with him, so it's better that we split before I go."

Huh — I didn't think anyone would need a holiday romance to have fun in the Caribbean. Just being there would be great. Much better than the week in a caravan in rain-soaked Britain that my family had planned. Honestly — some people had all the luck!

April came back from her holiday with an even better tan, loads of new clothes, and photos of the hunky boys she'd met there. It was obvious she must have had a great time.

Things just got better and better. She came top in our half-yearly assessments at school and she had a host of boys from school hanging around her asking her out.

And then, to cap it all, April came into school one morning with even more exciting news.

"I'll be leaving here at the end of the week," she told our form teacher casually. "I'm going to live in London."

London! With its bright lights, shops, trendy discos and pop stars everywhere. I'd have given my eye teeth to live there. But, as usual, it was April who had all the luck — not me.

I was feeling so angry and fed up that at lunchtime I decided to go for a walk by myself. But it was cold outside, so I stopped off at the cloakroom to get my coat. And that's when I heard April — sobbing to another girl, Patsy.

I couldn't believe it at first. What did April have to cry about? She had everything going for her. Then I listened and I realised . . .

"It's happened at last," she was saying. "Mum and Dad have decided to split up. I knew they would. They haven't got on for years."

"Which one are you going to live with?" Patsy asked.

"Neither," April replied miserably. "They don't want me — they never have. They're both too wrapped up in their own careers and social lives to be interested in anything *I* do.

"Do you know," she continued, "even on holiday they go off for business meetings and I get left to hang around the hotel on my own. It's awful!"

"So who will you be living with in London?" Patsy asked.

"My gran," April sobbed. "But she doesn't really want me either. I heard her telling Mum so. I'll just be a nuisance in her house — like I've always been with Mum and Dad. Nobody in my family cares about me, Patsy. Oh, I'm so miserable!"

I crept away then. I didn't need to hear any more. I'd finally realised that April wasn't a person to be envied at all.

Sure, she had lots of material things — clothes, foreign holidays, a nice house, a pony, and all that. But she didn't have the most important things of all — her parents' love. *She* didn't have someone she could turn to and depend on, like I did.

And I knew then that I'd never ever moan about my own life again, because I'd finally realised how very lucky I was. And I wouldn't envy April any more either. Instead, I'd just feel sorry for her . . .

continued from page 84.

# too old! PART FOUR

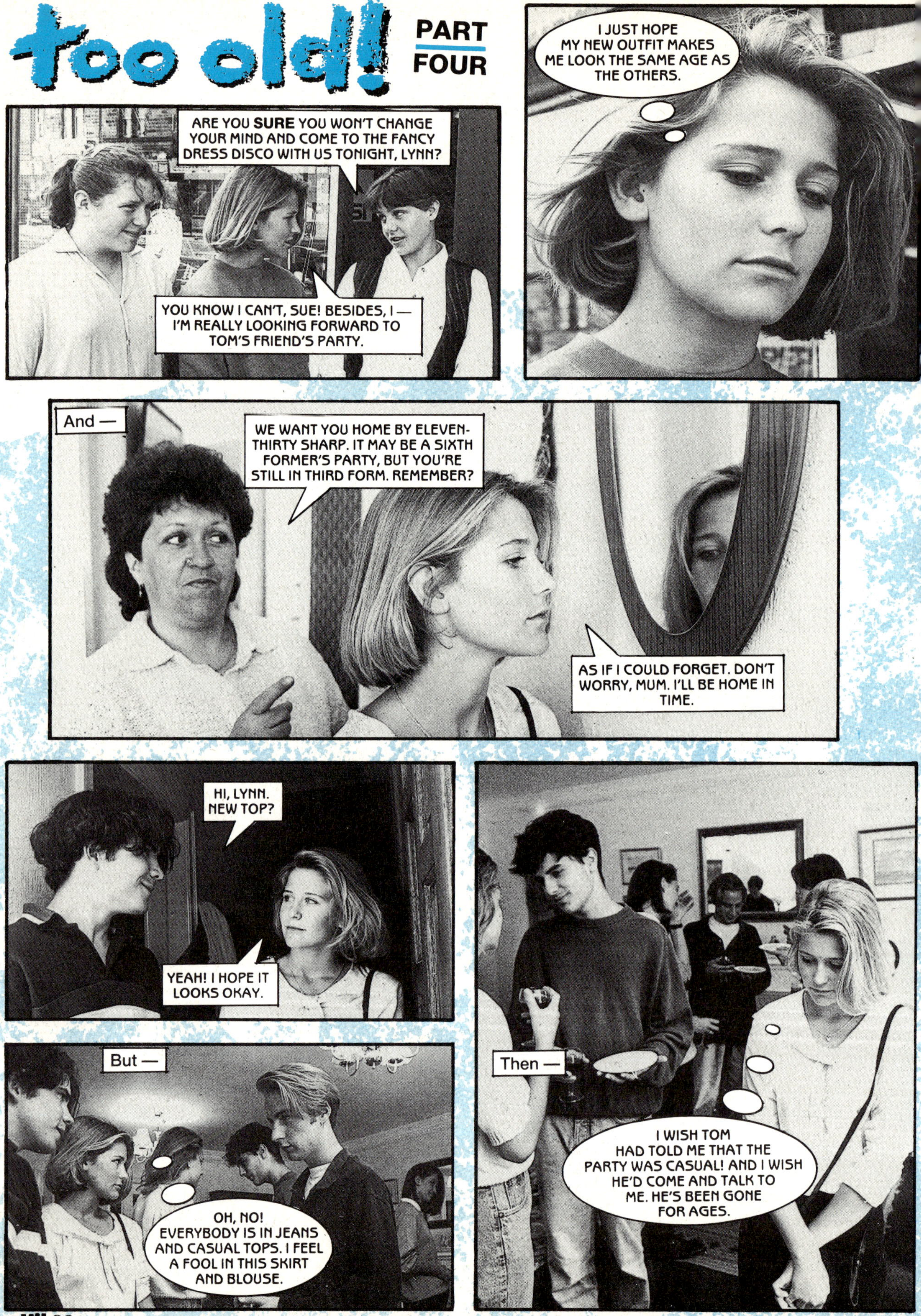

AT LAST! WHERE'VE YOU BEEN?
JUST TALKIN' TO DAN. HEY, WHAT'S THE MATTER, LYNN? WE'RE AT A PARTY — SUPPOSED TO BE HAVING FUN!
HE DOESN'T UNDERSTAND. IF I WAS WITH MY OWN MATES I'D BE HAVIN' A GREAT TIME. BUT I FEEL STUPID HERE.
Later —
I KNOW THIS HASN'T BEEN A LOAD OF LAUGHS FOR YOU, LYNN, BUT I'M GLAD YOU CAME. YOU'RE REALLY SPECIAL.
AND SO ARE YOU, TOM. BUT — BUT IT'S ABOUT TIME I STARTED FOR HOME.
NO PROBLEM. YOUR COAT'S UPSTAIRS.
OKAY. WON'T BE LONG.
EVERYONE'S WONDERING HOW YOU MANAGED TO CATCH TOM, LYNN. I MEAN, YOU'RE QUITE PRETTY — BUT JUST A KID. HE COULD HAVE ANY SIXTH FORM GIRL HE WANTED.
OH, I — I . . .
THIS IS AWFUL! THEY'RE NOTHING BUT A BUNCH OF CATS!
And —
'NIGHT, LYNN. I'LL CALL IN TOMORROW AFTERNOON. OKAY?
SURE.
THIS CAN'T GO ON! I — I'VE GOT TO DO SOMETHING.

So, next day —
I THOUGHT ABOUT IT ALL NIGHT, TOM, BUT I DIDN'T CHANGE MY MIND. I LIKE YOU A LOT, BUT IT JUST WON'T WORK.
YOU — YOU COULD BE RIGHT. I STILL THINK YOU'RE SPECIAL, LYNN, BUT I'VE BEEN THINKING, TOO. WE JUST DON'T HAVE MUCH IN COMMON, DO WE?
On Monday —
HI, LYNN. THE DISCO WAS BRILLIANT! HOW WAS YOUR PARTY?
ROTTEN! AND I MIGHT AS WELL TELL YOU, TOM AND I HAVE FINISHED!
WHAT? AND I THOUGHT IT WAS THE ROMANCE OF THE CENTURY.
SO DID I — TO BEGIN WITH. BUT YOU LOT WERE RIGHT. TOM IS TOO OLD FOR ME. HIS MATES ALL TREATED ME LIKE A SILLY KID AND — AND I JUST COULDN'T FIT IN!
At break —
LYNN! IS IT TRUE THAT YOU'VE FINISHED WITH TOM? YOU MUST BE CRAZY!
NOT AS CRAZY AS YOU THINK, FRAN.
WATCH YOUR LANGUAGE
I JUST WISH AN OLDER GUY WOULD ASK ME OUT. IT'D BE SO EXCITING AND DIFFERENT.
A BIT TOO DIFFERENT, IF YOU ASK ME.
YET IT WAS EXCITING! BUT THE TRUTH IS I COULDN'T COPE. I KNOW I'VE DONE THE RIGHT THING — EVEN THOUGH IT HURTS LIKE MAD!
THE END

# GET BUSY

## Things to do when you've got a spare hour.

Do *all* your homework for the week, leaving you free for fun.

Write a letter to a long lost pal.

Put on your fave viddie then relax with your hot choc and toast. Aaah, bliss!

Practise your funky dance moves so you can wow the local posse at the next rave.

Repair or alter any clothes in need of attention. Amazing! You've expanded your wardrobe in one easy step!

Tape all your fave songs so you've got a happenin' party tape for good sounds wherever you go.

Make an extra spesh fancy card for someone's birthday or Christmas.

Do your nails so they're posh and shiny.

Go swimming — it's the best form of exercise you can do. And if you can't swim — *learn!*

Okay, so it's boring, but you could tidy your room 'till its nice 'n' sparkly clean. Just think of all the extra Brownie points you'll earn from the parents. This could go a long way towards getting you those new jeans you've been after.

Think out a fail safe plan to capture the heart of that hunky lad you lurrve sooo much. Now *that's* time well spent.

See how many hilarious faces you can make at yourself in the mirror.

Try out some new make-up looks.

Work out how old you are in hours, minutes and seconds. Argh!

Look out old family photos and have a laugh at mum 'n' dad in their 'trendy' gear and your bruv in the bath when he was two (keep this one for embarrassing him when his girlfriend comes round).

Treat yourself to a double helping of ice cream with chocolate flakes, strawberry sauce and wafers.

Give your dog a bath (warn all in the vicinity first!), clean out the goldfish bowl and the hamster cage. Phew!

Play Scrabble or Ludo with your best mate, make up your own rules and end up having a pillow fight. Yeah, it's daft, but what are friends for?

Chuck out every pair of holey tights you own so that there's no frantic scrabbling for a hole-free pair the next time you need some.

Look through your mum's latest catalogue and decide what you'd like if you could have *anything!*

Check out some old Hi! mags for fabsy beauty treatments that'll have you looking and feeling great!

Find out which star sign you are compatible with and see if you know any lads who you'd get on with.

# BRAIN STRAIN

POP CHICKS BEWARE — MUSO SCRAMBLES TO FRY YOUR MIND.

## DEF GEN(?)

**True or false —**

**1.** Betty Boo's real name is Alison Clarkson.
**2.** Adamski used to be a window cleaner and a gardener.
**3.** The Soupdragons are all brothers.
**4.** Kim Wilde was supporting act for Michael Jackson on his '89 tour.
**5.** Sinead O'Connor was once a kissogram girl.
**6.** George Michael owns a golden labrador called 'Hippy'.
**7.** Donnie 'New Kid' Wahlberg has been arrested on more than one occasion.
**8.** Jazzie B of Soul II Soul plans to open his own hospital(!) or an airline.
**9.** The Rebel MCs real name is Mike West.
**10.** Kylie Minogue has false teeth.

## TAKE A GUESS!

**1 Where do the New Kids hail from?**
**a** New York.
**b** Boston, Massachussets.
**c** Idaho.

**2 Sign O' The Times, Purple Rain and Grafitti Bridge are all albums by:**
**a** Bobby Brown.
**b** Whitney Houston.
**c** Prince.

**3 Which all girl band was Betty Boo a member of —**
**a** Bananarama.
**b** She Rockers.
**c** Wilson Philips.

**4 Who did Craig McLachlan write Amanda for?**
**a** Rachel Friend.
**b** Amanda De Cadanet.
**c** Dannii Minogue.

**5 Adamski's dog is called.**
**a** Rover.
**b** Sid.
**c** Dis.

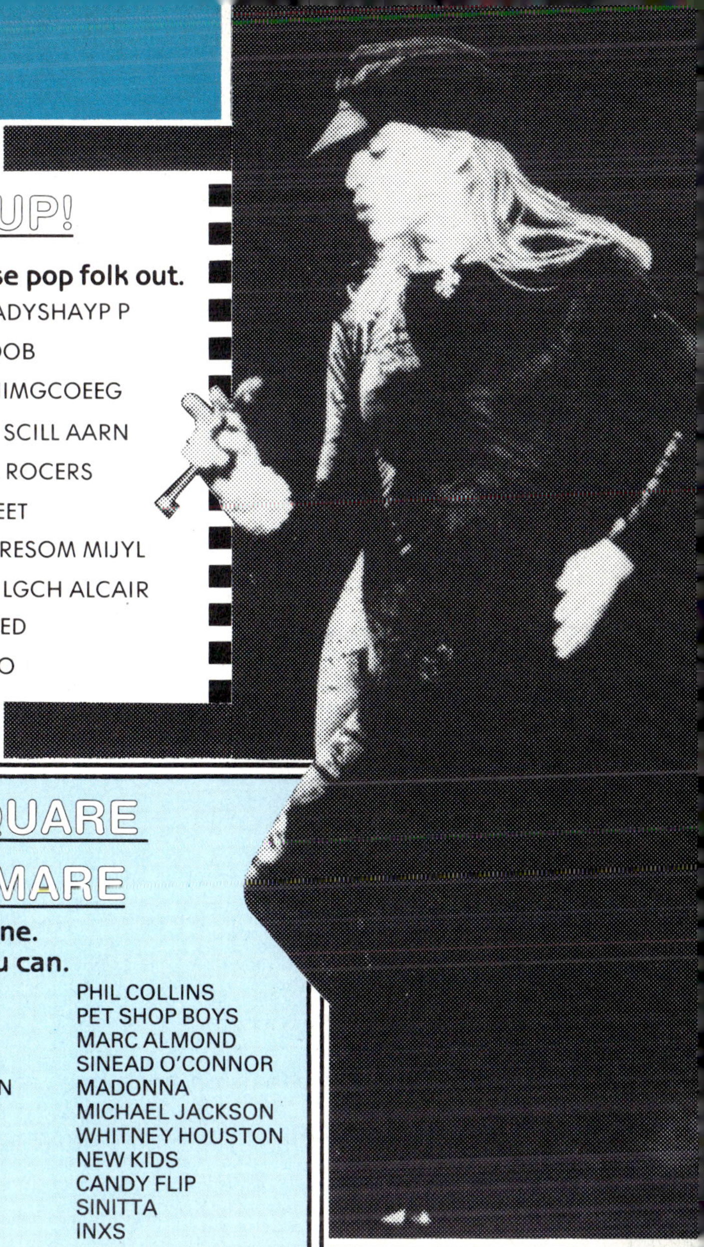

## MIX-UP!

**Sort these pop folk out.**

**1** NO MADYSHAYP P
**2** JIV NOOB
**3** REAL HIMGCOEEG
**4** DELBIE SCILL AARN
**5** MI PAL ROCERS
**6** TOX REET
**7** LIVEM RESOM MIJYL
**8** NAMC LGCH ALCAIR
**9** TILEE-EED
**10** NISPOO

## POPSQUARE NIGHTMARE

**Ha! An easy one.**
**Find 'em if you can.**

ADAMSKI
BANANARAMA
KYLIE
BIG FUN
JASON DONOVAN
SONIA
NENEH CHERRY
BELOVED
BETTY BOO
STONE ROSES
LINDY LAYTON
PHIL COLLINS
PET SHOP BOYS
MARC ALMOND
SINEAD O'CONNOR
MADONNA
MICHAEL JACKSON
WHITNEY HOUSTON
NEW KIDS
CANDY FLIP
SINITTA
INXS

| | | | | | | | | | | | | | | | |
|---|---|---|---|---|---|---|---|---|---|---|---|---|---|---|---|
| P | Z | W | L | I | N | D | Y | L | A | Y | T | O | N | X | T |
| H | I | H | O | D | N | O | M | L | A | C | R | A | M | L | M |
| I | M | I | C | H | A | E | L | J | A | C | K | S | O | N | A |
| L | L | T | A | A | T | T | I | N | I | S | C | R | N | A | D |
| C | C | N | A | I | N | O | S | I | E | D | O | P | E | M | O |
| O | S | E | B | L | M | N | O | S | Q | N | R | I | N | A | N |
| L | D | Y | I | N | X | S | O | O | N | U | B | L | E | R | N |
| L | I | I | C | B | A | H | P | O | U | K | E | F | H | A | A |
| I | K | O | L | K | E | U | G | O | Y | V | L | Y | C | N | N |
| N | W | U | J | N | V | O | R | L | O | W | O | D | H | A | A |
| S | E | S | O | T | D | S | I | C | C | A | V | N | E | N | B |
| G | N | T | F | A | S | E | M | P | Y | R | E | A | R | A | I |
| D | S | O | E | A | D | A | M | S | K | I | D | C | R | B | G |
| Y | H | N | K | P | E | T | S | H | O | P | B | O | Y | S | F |
| X | I | O | U | O | O | B | Y | T | T | E | B | S | E | T | U |
| S | Y | J | A | S | O | N | D | O | N | O | V | A | N | X | N |

## ANSWERS

**MIX UP!**
**1.** Happy Mondays.
**2.** Bon Jovi.
**3.** George Michael.
**4.** Belinda Carlisle.
**5.** Proclaimers.
**6.** Roxette.
**7.** Jimmy Somerville.
**8.** Craig McLachlan.
**9.** Deee-Lite.
**10.** Poison.

**TAKE A GUESS!**
**1.** B. **2.** C. **3.** B. **4.** A. **5.** C.

**DEF GEN(?)**
**1.** I. **2.** T. **3.** F. **4.** T. **5.** T.
**6.** T. **7.** T. **8.** T. **9.** T. **10.** F.

# Missing You

SEE YOU NEXT WEEK THEN, KAREN.
'BYE, LEE. ENJOY YOUR CAMPING!
COME ON, LEE. WE'LL MISS THE BUS!
RIGHT. JUST COMING, BILL.
I NEARLY FORGOT! HERE'S YOUR MAGAZINE. I TOOK IT HOME BY MISTAKE!
I WONDERED WHERE THAT WAS!
LEE'S A HOOT. HE PRETENDS NOT TO, BUT HE READS MY "HI!" EVERY WEEK!
Later—
IT'S GOING TO BE A LONG WEEK WITHOUT HIM. OH, WHAT'S THIS? ARE YOU HAPPY WITH YOUR PARTNER? THAT LOOKS INTERESTING!

HUH — TYPICAL! IT'S BEEN FILLED IN! OH, LEE — YOU COULD'VE LEFT **ME** SOMETHING TO DO!
Then she took a closer look.
QUESTION ONE. DOES YOUR PARTNER ALWAYS LOOK THEIR BEST? ANSWER — VERY RARELY! WELL, THAT'S NOT VERY NICE!
CRUMBS. MAYBE I SHOULDN'T READ ANY MORE OF THIS. THE WHOLE QUIZ HAS BEEN FILLED IN . . .
But, in her room—
IT'S NO USE — I'LL HAVE TO SEE WHAT ELSE HE'S PUT! QUESTION TWO — IS YOUR PARTNER SOMETIMES TOO POSSESSIVE? OH, NO! HE'S TICKED THE YES BOX!
Karen thought back—
IT'S ONLY A WEEK'S BREAK WITH MY MATES, KAREN — A BIT OF CAMPING!
IT'S JUST THAT I'LL MISS YOU SO MUCH, LEE.
WHAT IF HE FINDS ANOTHER GIRL WHILE HE'S AWAY?
WHAT ELSE? QUESTION SIX. IS YOUR PARTNER EVER BORING? HE'S TICKED THE YES BOX AGAIN. HE — HE THINKS I'M BORING!

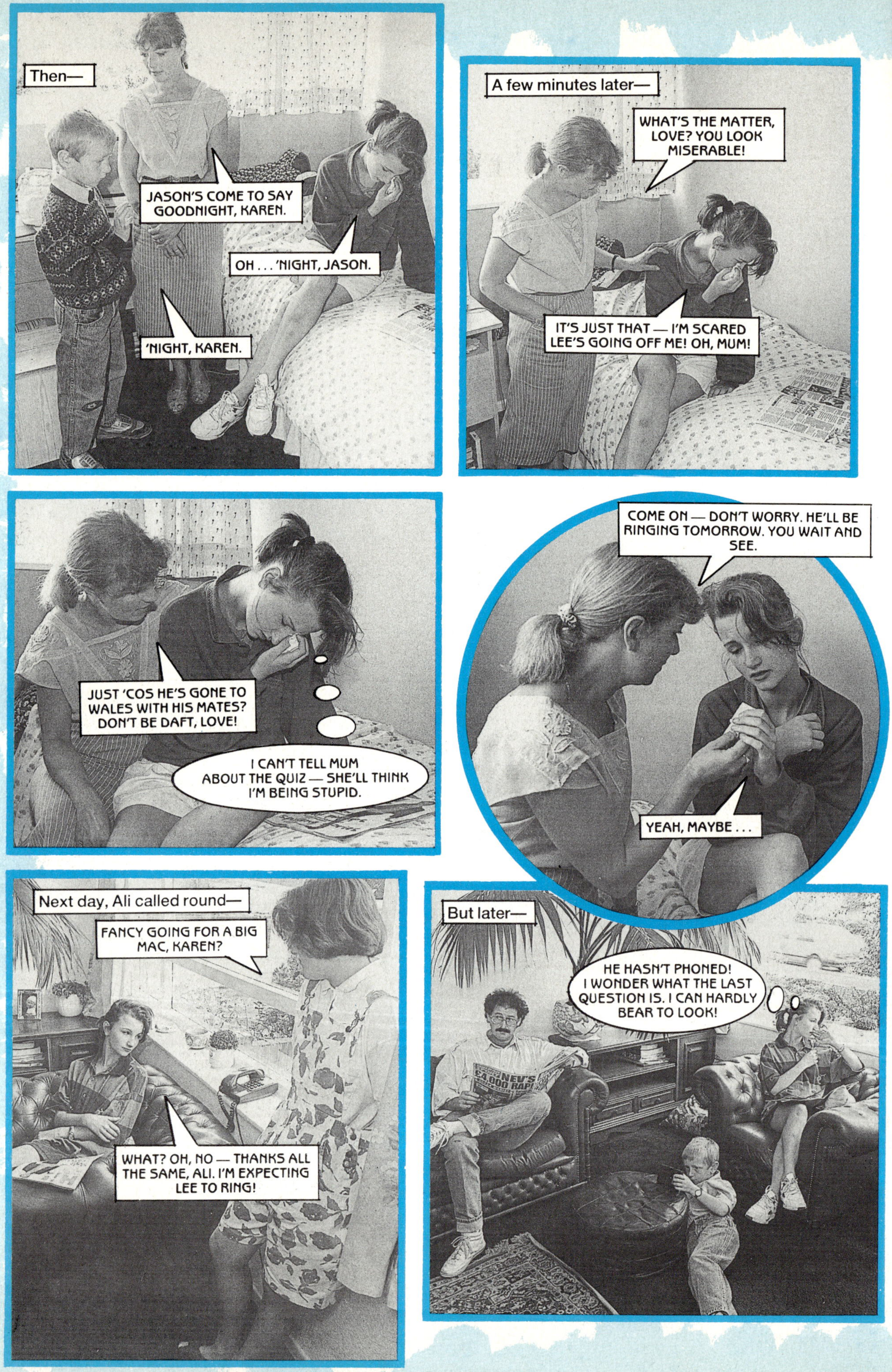
Then—
JASON'S COME TO SAY GOODNIGHT, KAREN.
OH . . . 'NIGHT, JASON.
'NIGHT, KAREN.
A few minutes later—
WHAT'S THE MATTER, LOVE? YOU LOOK MISERABLE!
IT'S JUST THAT — I'M SCARED LEE'S GOING OFF ME! OH, MUM!
JUST 'COS HE'S GONE TO WALES WITH HIS MATES? DON'T BE DAFT, LOVE!
I CAN'T TELL MUM ABOUT THE QUIZ — SHE'LL THINK I'M BEING STUPID.
COME ON — DON'T WORRY. HE'LL BE RINGING TOMORROW. YOU WAIT AND SEE.
YEAH, MAYBE . . .
Next day, Ali called round—
FANCY GOING FOR A BIG MAC, KAREN?
WHAT? OH, NO — THANKS ALL THE SAME, ALI. I'M EXPECTING LEE TO RING!
But later—
HE HASN'T PHONED! I WONDER WHAT THE LAST QUESTION IS. I CAN HARDLY BEAR TO LOOK!

HAVE YOU EVER WISHED YOU'D NEVER MET? AND — AND LEE'S MARKED **THAT** YES BOX WITH A GREAT BIG CROSS!
WHAT AM I GONNA DO? OH, LEE — I THOUGHT WE WERE SO HAPPY!
ARE YOU ALL RIGHT, LOVE?
Then—
AUNTIE SHIRLEY'S HERE TO LOOK AFTER JASON. YOUR DAD AND I ARE POPPING OUT FOR AN HOUR, KAREN.
OH — RIGHT, MUM.
OH, KAREN — I'M SORRY IF I SPOILT YOUR MAGAZINE, LOVE. ONLY I FILLED IN A QUIZ ABOUT UNCLE JIM, WHEN I BABYSAT THE OTHER DAY.
U-UNCLE JIM? YOU — YOU MEAN IT WAS **YOU** WHO DID THE QUIZ?
YES, WELL, WE'D HAD A BIT OF A ROW, AND I THOUGHT I'D LET OFF STEAM! AREN'T YOU GOING TO ANSWER THAT PHONE?
IT **WASN'T** LEE AT ALL! HE DOESN'T THINK ALL THOSE THINGS ABOUT ME!
In fact—
HI, KAREN. I HAD TO RING — I'M REALLY MISSING YOU!
NOT — NOT HALF AS MUCH AS I'M MISSING YOU, LEE!
FROM NOW ON I'M GONNA **HIDE** MY COPY OF "HI!"!
THE END

# JILL'S PHOTO FILE

It's always very difficult when your best friend moves away. You feel as if part of yourself is missing! But you'll never make a new best friend by sitting around feeling sorry for yourself. Get out and about — join in things at school, and above all — be friendly. You've got to give a little in order to receive. I'm sure you'll make a new best friend soon.

# 50 WAYS TO MAKE CHRISTMAS MERRY!

**Get together with a few mates and stand on the street corner giving out crackers to people who pass by.**

When you've finished all your shopping, put your loose cash in the nearest charity bottle. It'll make you feel *really* good!

**Talk Mum into using paper plates for Christmas dinner. Okay, so it won't be so posh — but think of the time you'll save on the washing up!**

Get up mega early on Christmas morning and spray "snow" all over Mum and Dad's bedroom window. When they wake up they'll think it's a white Christmas. Mind you, it won't be so much fun if they make you spend all day scraping it off again.

**Get up mega early (again) and swap all the labels on the Christmas presents. It'll be a *hoot* when Dad tries to say he's thrilled with his New Kids Album and Mum goes ecstatic over her pipe!**

Arrange a party and invite everyone you know. Ask permission first, though, or it could be a disaster.

**Dig out your old kiddies' poetry book and read "The Night Before Christmas". It's brill!**

Wear lots of red, green and white. That's *dead* Christmassy!

**Make mince pies!**

Sprinkle glitter in your hair before you go to any parties. That way you're *sure* to outshine all the other girls there.

**Have a treasure hunt. Hide little presents all over the house and leave clues so everyone has to search for their pressies.**

Have a go at making marzipan fruits. They're great fun to make and even *more* fun to eat!

**Dress up as a snowman and stand in the front garden. This is brilliant for a giggle — especially if there isn't any snow around.**

Send the guy you fancy an extra special, slushy card — and sign it! It might just give him the push he needs.

**Get together with your mates and put on a pantomime. Draw the cast out of a hat though, 'cos everybody'll want to be Cinderella and nobody'll fancy being an ugly sister!**

Wrap tinsel round the dog's collar. After all, why should *he* be left out!

**Wear tinsel "scrunchies" in your hair and hang Christmas tree deccies from your ears. You may feel a fool — but it'll give all your mates a good laugh!**

Do all your Christmas shopping early. Rushing round the shops at five o'clock on Christmas Eve is guaranteed to kill *all* Christmas spirit!

**Put tinsel round all your favourite posters. We can assure you that Tom Cruise looks even *more* gorgeous with a glittery halo.**

Get some green and red nail varnish and paint holly on your nails.

**Buy one of these mega cheap, mass produced tapes of American Christmas songs and play it all day. It'll make your house feel like the shopping mall — but without the crowds!**

Make a "cake" from bread crumbs, nuts, oatmeal and fat and put it out for the birds on Christmas Day.

**Buy the biggest stocking you can find to hang up on Christmas Eve.**

Persuade your teachers to wear party hats in class on the last day of term. If they refuse, then *you* wear a party hat.

**Play charades — you know, "Give Us A Clue"! That's always good for a laugh at Christmas.**

Use Christmas as an excuse to pig out! You can worry about losing weight *after* the festive season.

**Put up a Christmas Tree in *every* room of the house! It may be messy — but it'll sure look bright! And if *you* do the decorating, you'll get to eat all the choccie deccies!**

Make up your own words to "The Twelve Days Of Christmas". It'll be easier in the long run, anyway, 'cos we don't know *anyone* who can remember *all* the words of that song.

**Search the house for all your old board games. Christmas Day is the ideal time to play with these and *all* the family can join in!**

Use tinsel and mistletoe to make yourself a pair of totally way out "deely-boppers" (you know, these silly space antennae things that stick up in the air and wobble about)!

**Decorate the rubber plant! In fact, decorate *all* the house plants.**

**Get a group of mates together and go carol singing in aid of your favourite charity. As long as you wear loads of woollies to keep warm you'll have a ball.**

Turn your bedroom into Santa's grotto. It'll make a change from the *grotty* mess it is during the rest of the year.

**Read your "Hi!" Annual — at least twice!**

Teach your budgie to sing Jingle Bells. If you haven't got a budgie, teach your goldfish (!).

**Be different! Organise a Hallowe'en party!**

Don't forget to write a list and send it to Santa. His address is The North Pole. Don't bother with a Stamped Addressed Envelope, though, 'cos he'll be busy at this time of year, so he's not likely to reply.

**Get yourself a pet reindeer! If this isn't possible, ask the dog to grow antlers!!!**

Send Liz a Christmas Card.

**Carry a sprig of mistletoe with you at *all* times — just in case you meet a hunk!**

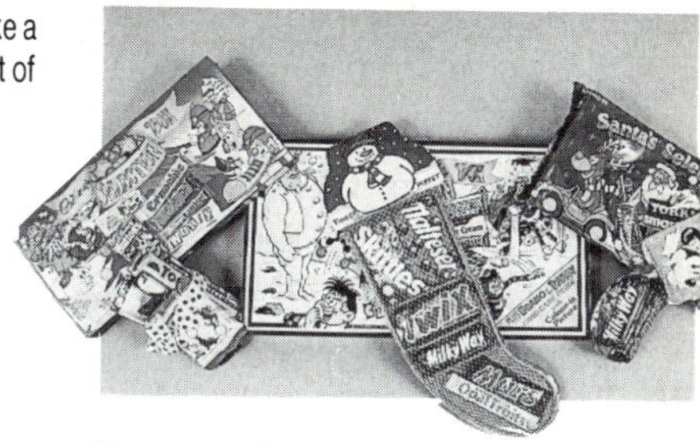

**Treat yourself to a mega selection box. This is the only time of year you can find them — and they're fabby!**

Get your chimney swept! Don't want Santa to get dirty, do we? If you don't have a chimney, get someone to give your central heating a service.

**Take your little bruv or sis (or your friend's little bruv or sis) to the local pantomime! You'll probably enjoy it more than them — and you might even get a sweetie!!**

Stick a cushion up Dad's jumper and ask him to go around saying "Ho, ho, ho!".

**Make snowballs out of cotton wool and have a snowball fight! This is not nearly as cold, wet *or* painful as the real thing!**

**Say Merry Christmas to people in the street. It's sure to cheer them up and it'll make you feel happy, too.**

Hire all the Christmas vids you can afford and spend the weekend before Christmas watching them. The older and slushier they are, the better. (Suggestion: White Christmas, Holiday Inn, Miracle on 34th Street, anything with Doris Day, etc.)

**Ring bells! Okay, so it might annoy the neighbours, but it'll give you *loads* of Chrimbo spirit! Ding, Dong! Ding, Dong!**

Set a jigsaw on a table. This is a great idea over Christmas as everyone can do a bit when they have some spare time. But remember to hide a piece before you start. That way *you* can be sure of putting in the very last piece.

**Be good! After all, Santa only comes to good girls or boys and we certainly don't want to miss out on a visit from *him*, do we?**

I SAY, I SAY, I SAY!
Oh, no — I've dropped my contact lens!
My other bike's a Harley Davidson!
Yesterday the cabbage patch, tomorrow the world!
No more photos — you'll have to speak to my agent!
Who said it was as easy as riding a bike?!
You put your right hoof in, your right hoof out . . .
Hangin' tough!
Oh, please — gimme a kiddy back!

Hi!
johnny depp
H

# YOU'VE GOT IT MADE!

**Don't stick to the same boring colours all the time. We show you how to party with these groovy make-up looks.**

## 1. RED ALERT

***If you're darker you can get away with stronger colours. Here's how to look hot, hot, hot!***

**BASE:** Light covering of foundation dusted with translucent or bronzing powder.

**EYES:** Use gold to highlight the browbone. Take dark reddy rust over the eyelids and very lightly along the lower lashes (you don't want to look ill!). Blend soft chocolate eyeliner along the lower lashes and smudge a tiny bit on to the outer corners of the eyelids. Two coats of black mascara.

**CHEEKS:** Rusty copper blusher.

**LIPS:** Bright red with gold pearl.

## 2. MISS MISTLETOE

***Be Christmas kissy in red and green. Suitable for any colouring.***

**BASE:** Pale foundation set with translucent powder.
**EYES:** Pale green (not too pearly) brushed over the eyelids and right up to the browbone. Soft mossy green blended over the eyelids. Darker, smoky green at the outer corners and along the lower lashes. Two coats of black mascara.
**CHEEKS:** Soft peachy blusher.
**LIPS:** The brightest red you can find.

## 3. HEAVY METAL

***Go for warm shimmering golds if you're dark.***

**BASE:** Light covering of foundation set with very light dusting or bronzing powder.
**EYES:** Light, sparkling gold brushed all over the eyelids. Bronzy rust applied to the outer corners and along lower lashes. Two coats of browny black mascara.
**CHEEKS:** Warm copper blusher.
**LIPS:** Copper metallic lipstick. Highlight the centre of your lips with a little dot of gold powder shadow.

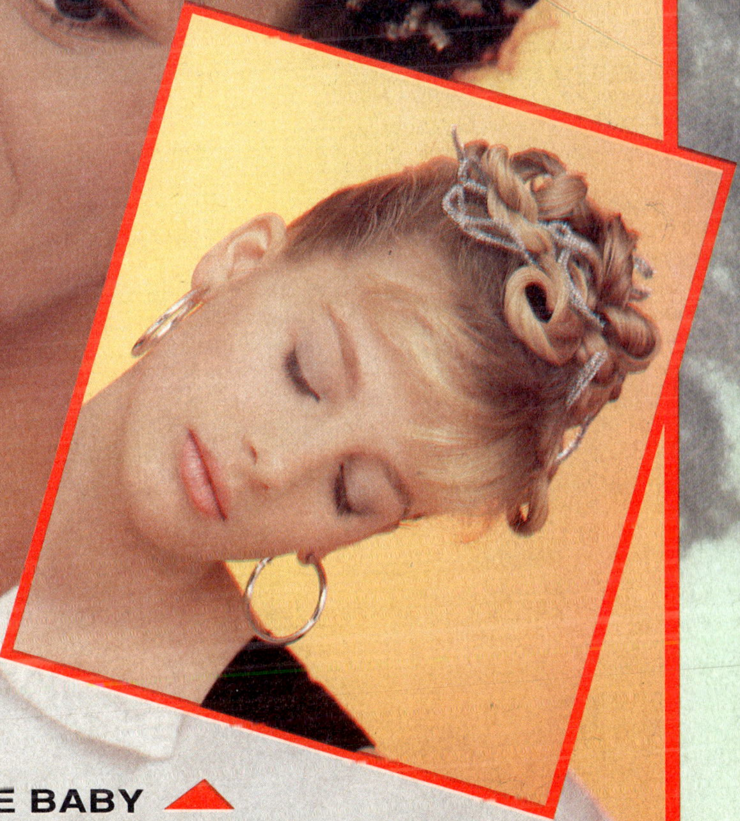

## 4. ICE ICE BABY

***If you're fair, pale silvery make-up can look great. So, for that Snow Queen look, here's what to do.***

**BASE:** A light pale foundation dusted over with translucent powder.
**EYES:** Soft silver or pale metallic grey all over the eyelid. Darker, smoky grey blended in at the outer corners. Soft violet grey smudged along the lower lashes. Two coats of dark grey mascara or one coat of black.
**CHEEKS:** A very light dusting of candy pink blusher.
**LIPS:** Pale pink lightly frosted lipstick.

# the only way is up!

**Would you believe our Liz started off as a waitress before reaching the dizzy heights of letter-opener for "Hi!"? And all your fave mega famous movie, music and TV peeps have had to do *their* share of boring or weird jobs, too . . .**

**Craig McLachlan had a right assortment of jobs before Ramsay Street, Summer Bay and Top Of The Pops beckoned — he worked as a plumber's mate, a brickie's mate, a body building coach and a model.**

Greg Benson and Sasha Mitchell used to be models, too.

**Liz's all-time fave, Tom Cruise, used to be a paper boy (long before "Hi!" started!). He also seriously considered entering the Priesthood! At the age of 14, he went to a Franciscan monastery school to train.**

Joe (New Kids) McIntyre used to earn extra dosh raking up leaves in neighbourhood gardens and helping out in a grocery store after school and at weekends.

**David Hasselhoff used to be a waiter. He also started his acting career in TV ads.**

Andy Crane and Simon Parkin started off as radio DJ's. And Andi Peters was a DJ for Top Man, doing the background 'sounds'!

**Neil Buchanan used to play guitar in a rock band called Marseilles — in fact, the TV Ed's got one of their albums!**

Betty Boo used to stock shelves in Marks and Sparks.

**Guy Pearce once held the title Teenage Mr Victoria — a junior muscle man no less!**

Peter O'Brien used to be a science teacher. Bet lotsa girlies had a crush on *this* teacher!

**Mel Gibson was *going* to be a chef or journalist before being accepted for drama college.**

Caron Keating worked as a waitress and shop assistant.

**Craig Thomson (Home and Away) had previous jobs as a greenkeeper, a dustbin man and an amateur boxer.**

Clint Boon (Inspiral Carpets) used to be a director of a furniture company which went bust!

**Phillip Schofield once worked as an ice-cream salesman in Newquay. Then he went on to become a mobile disco DJ.**

Madonna started off working as a waitress in Dunkin' Donuts — an American takeaway chain that sells coffee and doughnuts.

**Matthew Broderick's first love was soccer but he had to retire from the sport after an injury. Then he got into acting.**

Jon Bon Jovi worked in a junk yard, a fast food joint . . . and a shoe shop — bet you wouldn't feel hassled if *he* asked if you needed assistance.

**Emilio Estevez used to work as a janitor in a sports club, cleaning out showers and suchlike!**

Adamski was originally a window cleaner and then a gardener.

**Gloria Estefan worked as a Spanish and French interpreter at an American airport's customs department.**

Between acting jobs, Patrick Swayze worked as a carpenter to keep the dosh rolling in.

# Love Letter...

SARA had lost her homework . . .
WHAT A WALLY. MAYBE I'VE CHUCKED IT IN HERE BY MISTAKE WHEN I WAS CLEARING OUT MY BAG . . .
OH, WHAT'S THIS?
"DEAR SARAH, I'VE FANCIED YOU FOR AGES AND I REALLY WANT TO GO OUT WITH YOU . . ."
WOW! A SECRET ADMIRER. I WONDER WHO IT IS?
Later—
YOU CAN STOP WORRYING ABOUT YOUR HOMEWORK, 'COS YOU LEFT IT AT MY PLACE. AND I RECKON JON HARRIS WROTE THIS. IT LOOKS LIKE HIS WRITING.
OH, BRILLIANT, KELLY. JON'S REALLY NICE.
At home—
I REALLY WANT TO GO OUT WITH JON. THE ONLY THING IS . . .
HOW CAN I BE SURE THAT HE WROTE THIS NOTE? I'LL ASK KELLY WHAT SHE THINKS.

So—
WHAT'S THE PROBLEM? ALL YOU'VE GOT TO DO IS ASK HIM.
YEAH, I KNOW. BUT WHAT IF HE SAYS HE **DIDN'T** WRITE IT?
BUT WHAT IF HE SAYS HE DID? GO FOR IT, SARAH!
YEAH, YOU'RE RIGHT. I'LL ASK HIM WHEN I GET A CHANCE.
OH, WELL — HERE GOES . . .
ER, JON. I WAS — ER — WONDERING IF YOU WROTE THIS.
UM . . . NO, NOT GUILTY!
BUT HOW ABOUT IF I HELP YOU FIND OUT WHO DID?
OH, EM, THANKS!
CRIKEY — THIS IS SO EMBARRASSING. I FEEL A PROPER NERD!
RIGHT — ALL WE'VE GOT TO DO IS TO COMPARE THIS LETTER WITH SOME OF THE BOYS' HANDWRITING IN OUR CLASS.
OKAY, JON — LEAD ON!
So, later—
WHAT ABOUT THIS ONE? THEY ALMOST MATCH, DON'T THEY?
YEAH, ALMOST — BUT NOT QUITE. IT'S PAUL GIBBS, ISN'T IT?

YUGH! WELL, I'M GLAD **HE** DIDN'T WRITE THE NOTE ANYWAY!
THERE'S STILL A FEW BOOKS TO CHECK OUT, SARAH. WE'LL FIND HIM, DON'T WORRY.
But at the end of the lesson—
IT'S STRANGE. WE'VE MANAGED TO CHECK OUT EVERYBODY AND THE HANDWRITING ON MY NOTE DOESN'T MATCH ANYBODY'S.
WAIT A MINUTE. THERE'S A BOOK HERE. HEY, IT MATCHES THE NOTE!
I DON'T BELIEVE IT! IT'S JON'S EXERCISE BOOK! WHAT'S HE PLAYING AT?
Then—
SO YOU'VE FOUND ME OUT. SORRY, SARAH!
WHAT'S GOING ON? ARE YOU TRYING TO MAKE A FOOL OF ME OR SOMETHING?
N-NO, OF COURSE NOT. I JUST LOST MY BOTTLE WHEN YOU ASKED IF IT WAS ME. I THOUGHT MAYBE IF WE SPENT SOME TIME TOGETHER I MIGHT GET UP THE NERVE TO ASK YOU OUT.
OH, I SEE!
SO — EM — WOULD YOU LIKE TO COME SKATING WITH ME ON SATURDAY?
I THOUGHT YOU'D NEVER ASK!
THE END

# THE WRITE STUFF!

**What does your handwriting say about you? Just take a peek at these star scribblings and all will be revealed . . . well, almost all!**

The fact that Pip's capital letters are so much longer than the rest of his letters shows that once he's made up his mind it's almost impossible to get him to change it. Underlining his signature shows he's self-confident, enthusiastic and bubbly. He can also keep a secret and is very ambitious, but nice with it.

Kylie's large, fluid signature shows someone who's impulsive, happy-go-lucky and thinks a lot of herself. The fact that her writing gets bigger as it goes on means she's honest and sincere and the missing dots from her 'i's indicate she's very independent and self-sufficient — in fact, a bit of a rebel! Handwriting as upright as this shows a thoughtful and self-controlled person who can be a bit unfriendly till you get to know her.

The most straightforward of the bunch, that's Jonathan, whose underlined signature shows he's self-confident and enthusiastic. He's someone you can trust with all your secrets and he's fun, too! Truthful and slightly sensitive, he's generous and down-to-earth despite all his fame 'n' fortune!

The way Andy's simplified his first name shows he's a pretty clever chappie who's keen to save time. The fact his signature's very upright means he's thoughtful but can be a little difficult to approach. Writing that decreases in size like this shows he could have a slightly cunning side, but the fact that he's written his whole name shows he's usually fairly open.

What does this signature tell us about Garth Pillow . . . or should that be Marti Pellow? Well, the pressure and forward slant of his writing show he's a confident chappie who's very active and outgoing. Sociable, he's bound to have loads of chums and right in the limelight is where he loves to be. (We can tell that from the size of his signature.) He can be a little big-headed, but he makes such a loyal friend that people who know him won't really mind this.

Illegible signatures like this (Donnie Wahlberg) indicate that the writer thinks he's superior to you and reckons the short time he's taken to scrawl his signature is all he can spare you. Yikes! However, the *rest* of his writing reveals he's someone who's pretty honest and well-balanced. Whew!

This writing doesn't give much away, but the illustration Danny's made from his signature *does.* An easy-going guy with a great sense of humour, he's always on the move! The upright lettering shows he can be a bit cool as does the fact that he's the only one to have written his signature in capitals.

Sinitta's another person who *appears* outgoing and confident, but her liking for black ink shows she's actually desperate not to be misunderstood. This is also shown in her circular 'i' dots — she wants to be regarded as sophisticated and socially aware. A brill, funny friend, Snit would never ever reveal a secret, but look out if she doesn't get what she wants. There'll be trouble!

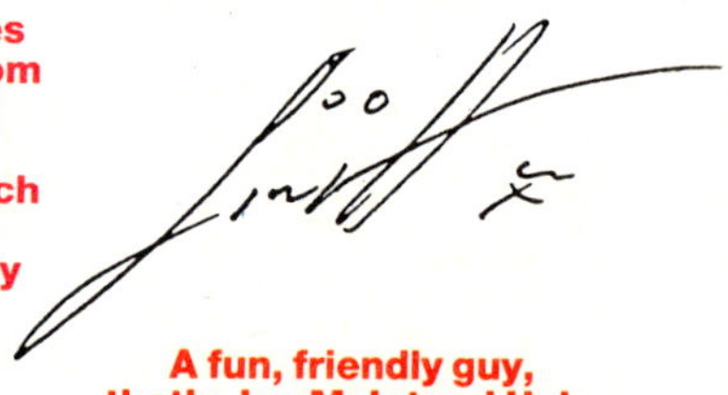

A fun, friendly guy, that's Joe McIntyre! He's also rather sensitive (aw, petal!) and very well-balanced. He'll tell you the truth if you ask his opinion and expect the same in return. A way to upset him is not to be punctual and pretend to be something you're not. Be warned.

What can we tell you about Jase? Well, he's popular, open, enthusiastic and charming. But he's also very anxious not to be misunderstood — the fact that he overwrites his 'o's shows this. Down to earth, despite his fame and fortune, Jase likes to be in control and is very easy-going — as long as things go his way. Oh, and he'd never ever betray you.

Jase

Elaborate writing like this shows someone who fancies himself *or* (don't get all huffy just yet) someone who wants to hide a little of himself. The strange mix of capitals and lower case could indicate that Jordan's careless and so busy thinking ahead he tends to overlook things. Unfortunately, using a star to dot his 'i' and putting *his* name in quotes, makes it highly likely the first half of our first sentence *is* true. (Sorry!)

Love Always & Forever, "Jordan Knight"

Craig McLachlan's happy-go-lucky and impulsive but hates to waste time — the fact that he hasn't bothered giving his 'g' a tail shows this. A bit forgetful at times, Craig's clever, outgoing and extremely popular. He'll always tell you what's on his mind and give an honest answer when asked his opinion.

Craig x

This person is talkative, argumentative, and can be a bit of a moan at times. However, she can be a very good friend too and is artistic, interesting and unable to resist temptation — especially when it's in the shape of a bar, block or triangle (of chocolate, that is!). And how do we know all this? 'Cos it's our own dear Liz, that's why!

Can I have a rise, please?

JOE McINTYRE

JORDAN

CRAIG McLACHLAN

PHILLIP SCHOFIELD

JONATHAN

MARTI PELLOW

DONNIE WAHLBERG

JASON DONOVAN

SINITTA

KYLIE MINOGUE

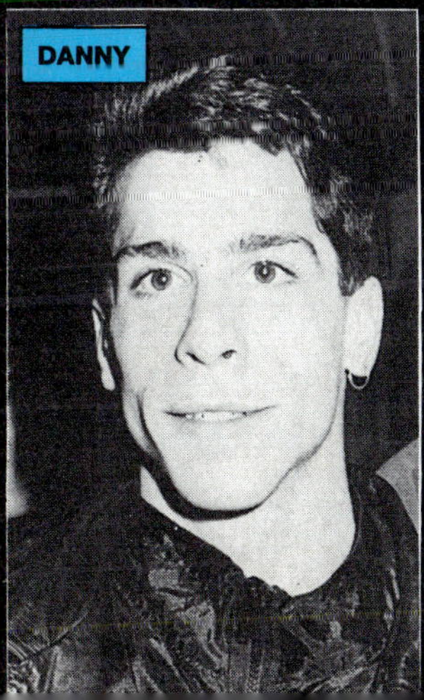
DANNY

ANDY CRANE

# ON LOC

**Okay, so you fancy being a model and spending your life posing elegantly on tropical beaches! Unfortunately, it isn't quite like that — as Susie, one of our favourite models, knows only too well!**

A COLD DAY IN MARCH, SOMEWHERE IN BRITAIN.

(A make-up artist finds herself called on to do *all* sorts of jobs.)

LATER THE SAME DAY

AND IT DOESN'T ONLY HAPPEN TO MODELS.

This took the Beauty Ed twenty minutes to set up . . .

. . . and the sea five seconds to knock down!

# ATION!

SOMETIMES A MODEL'S LIFE CAN BE DANGEROUS!
More action please, Susie.
Like this?
Or this?
Or this?
EEEEEEEK!
AND IT'S TOUGH WORK!
Faster, Susie! Don't let a little wind stop you!
I'm trying — honestly! But . . .
. . . I just seem to be . . .
. . . .going backwards!
BUT IT'S FUN TOO!
Hold tight!
Wheeeeee!!!
Humph! I want another go!

# IT'S A DOG'S LIFE

IT was Saturday evening. Martin was frying the chips and I was standing behind the counter, day-dreaming about what Mum and Dad were up to. I was picturing them eating their calamares in a little Greek taverna, when our first customer came in. He was a bit taller than me, with groovy blond hair and a pair of mischievous blue eyes.

"Hiya!"

He gave me a cheeky wink, before running his eyes down our price list. As he did so, a slim, black dog walked in and sat down behind him.

Martin noticed it too.

"Dogs aren't allowed in here," he told the boy bluntly.

I held my breath. With my six foot brother glaring at him, I thought the boy would quickly garble an apology and take the dog outside. But he didn't and I was impressed.

He looked at Martin for a second then turned round.

"Bill! Go on, out!" he said, pointing at the door.

"Sorry about that," the boy apologised, grinning up at Martin. "He must've got a whiff of your sausages!"

Martin grudgingly accepted the boy's apology and turned his attention back to the chips. The boy grinned at me before he gave the list another brief glance.

"Can I have a couple of cod, a portion of chips and," he paused to look at the cans of drink, ". . . and a coke please?"

I could feel myself growing hot under his gaze as I got his order. I told myself it was just the heat from the fryer.

"Em, what's your name by the way?" he asked, as he took a chip out of the bag and blew on it.

"Pippa," I replied, feeling my face go hot again.

Martin had stopped stirring the chips and I could tell he was listening.

"I'm Tim. See you next week then," he promised.

He popped the chip in his mouth and nonchalantly walked out.

I smiled to myself as I gazed after him. He was completely different to any boy I'd ever met before.

"Confident little beggar, isn't he?" Martin commented, from behind me, as we watched Tim go.

"Mmm — I suppose he is," I agreed, "and that's why I like him!"

On my way home from one of my usual spending sprees next Saturday morning, I went into the pet shop and bought some doggy chocs for Bill. After all, maybe the way to a boy's heart was through his dog's stomach!

Martin, and one of our regular customers, grumpy Mr Jenkins, were discussing the day's football results when Tim came into the shop that evening.

"How's you?" he asked cheerfully.

"Fine thanks," I said, thinking to myself how swoonsome he looked.

Then I remembered Bill and looked over to the doorway.

"Oh, what's Bill done?" I asked, as I noticed a bandage on one of his front paws.

"Cut his paw on a piece of glass on the beach, didn't you, you wally?" Tim explained, as he gave Bill's head an affectionate rub.

"Oh, you poor thing," I sympathised. "Never mind, these will make you feel better."

I took the chocs out of my apron pocket and gave Bill a handful.

"You'll be a friend for life now," Tim commented, as Bill greedily devoured them and then nudged me for more.

I felt Tim's eyes on me as I tipped some out of the packet and I turned to look at him. We were so close together that I could see flecks of purple in his eyes and the way his blonde eyelashes curled at the ends. I wished we could have stayed like that forever, but grumpy Mr Jenkins had to spoil it.

"You're blocking the doorway," he moaned as he left. "Honestly, kids

**When Mum and Dad take their annual holiday each October, me and Martin, my nineteen-year-old brother, are left in charge of their fish and chip shop. Which is great, except for one thing.**

**Martin likes to think he's in charge of me, too!**

these days . . ."

Tim patted Bill on the head and went over to the counter.

"Nice bloke," he commented, indicating Mr Jenkins' retreating figure with his head. "Now what shall we have tonight?"

He looked at the list again.

"Cod and chips and a sausage for Bill, please," he said.

I got his order, hating Mr Jenkins for breaking up what I was sure was the start of something wonderful. But I was about to get lucky!

"Erm — do you fancy coming out one night?" Tim asked, as he concentrated on salting his chips.

"That'd be nice," I said, trying to keep the glee out of my voice.

"Haven't you got a lot of homework to do this week?" Martin butted in.

I glared at him.

"Thursday's a good night," I suggested.

I'd usually got most of my work done by then and the shop was closed on Thursday's, so I knew Martin wouldn't need my help. However, Martin seemed determined to put Tim off and came and stood beside me.

"I'm afraid Pippa isn't allowed out with boys on her own," he said pointedly.

"Martin!" I exclaimed through gritted teeth.

I could have murdered him! He ignored the plea in my eyes to shut up and carried on.

"Her mum and dad prefer it if she goes out in a group."

It was true that Mum and Dad liked me to go out with others, but even *they* stretched the point sometimes. I looked at Tim under my eyelashes to see what his reaction was. Instead of appearing put off by what Martin had said, he was nodding his agreement.

"That's what I had in mind too," he said, which took Martin by surprise. "I thought we could make up a foursome with a couple of friends of mine, Ed and Lola."

Tim was amazing. He seemed to have an answer for everying. Even so, I was a little disappointed that he hadn't wanted it to be just the two of us in the first place.

Martin sighed. He was beaten.

"Well, in that case, I suppose it will be all right," he agreed reluctantly. "But she's got to be back before ten," he added, pointing a warning finger at Tim.

I raised my eyes to the ceiling as he walked away from us and Tim gave me an understanding wink.

"I'll be round at seven o'clock then. See ya," he called out with a wave.

"See ya," I copied.

I spent ages wondering what to wear on Thursday night. In the end I decided on my newest pair of jeans and my white denim jacket. As I tied my hair up in a navy scrunchie, I wondered what Ed and Lola would be like and hoped I'd get on with them.

The doorbell rang at seven and I called goodbye to Martin.

"Don't forget, back at ten," he warned.

"You look nice," Tim commented, as I shut the front door behind me.

I smiled then looked around for his friends.

"Where's Ed and Lola?"

"They're waiting round the corner," he said with a grin.

He took my hand and squeezed it affectionately and I knew it was going to be a fantastic first date.

When I got home, just on ten, Martin was watching telly.

"Have a good time?" he asked.

"Yeah, great, thanks," I said, as I threw myself down into one of the armchairs. "We had a walk along the beach, then we all went back to his house and watched a video."

Martin nodded.

"What were his friends like?"

"Great fun," I said, trying hard not to laugh.

I don't think Martin would have been very amused if he'd known that Ed and Lola were Bill's mum and dad!

# AND SO TO BED...

1. A relaxing read . . . and what better to feast the eyes on than wonderful, amazing, brilliant "Hi!"?!

2. Be crease-free! Make sure the school uniform gets the once over.

3. Forget tea and coffee at bedtime. Try a relaxing hot milky drink for plentiful zzzzzs!

4. No grotty make-up marks on the pillow, purlease! It's make-up take-off time.

**Don't just leap into your jim-jams and dive into bed! Take time out and prepare yourself for a blissful night's snoozing.**